CW00740897

CORRUPTION
AND THE
DESTINY OF ASIA

Syed Hussein Alatas

Prentice Hall (M) Sdn. Bhd.
and
Simon & Schuster (Asia) Pte. Ltd.

This revised edition published by
Prentice Hall (M) Sdn. Bhd.
11A Jalan PJS 7/19
Bandar Sunway
46150 Petaling Jaya
Selangor Darul Ehsan
Malaysia

©1999 Simon & Schuster (Asia) Pte Ltd
A division of Simon & Schuster International Group

All rights reserved. No part of this publication may be
reproduced, stored in a retrieval system, or transmitted, in
any form, or by any means, electronic, mechanical,
photocopying, recording or otherwise, without the prior
permission in writing from the publisher.

Printed in Malaysia

5 4 3 2 1   03 02 01 00 99

Perpustakaan Negara Malaysia Cataloguing-in-Publication Data

Alatas, Syed Hussein, 1928-
    Corruption and the destiny of Asia / Syed Hussein Alatas.
    Bibliography: p.
    Includes index
    ISBN 983-9236-08-3
    1. Political corruption--Asia. 2. Political corruption--Social
    aspects--Asia. 1. Title.
    364.1323

ISBN: 983-9236-08-3
ISBN: 983-9236-22-9 (India Reprint)
ISBN: 983-9236-23-7 (Philippines Reprint)

First edition published under the title
The Sociology of Corruption
in 1968 by Donald Moore Press Ltd, Singapore

Second edition published under the title
The Problem of Corruption
in 1986 by Times Book International, Singapore

Simon & Schuster (Asia) Pte Ltd, *Singapore*
Prentice Hall, Inc., Upper Saddle River, *New Jersey*
Prentice Hall Europe, *London*
Prentice Hall Canada Inc., *Toronto*
Prentice Hall of Australia Pty Limited, *Sydney*
Prentice Hall Hispanoamericana, S.A., *Mexico*

To Abu Dzar al-Ghifari (d. AD 653), who valiantly fought against corruption and died lonely in exile in the desert of Rabadha. The fountain of his spirit continues to gush forth the call for justice, waiting for it to become a powerful river in a world scorched by injustice and oppression. Those who die for a cause awaken to life the dead among the living.

CONTENTS

Man is freer than he is commonly thought to be. He is greatly dependent upon his environment, but not to the degree of being subjugated to it. The greater part of our destiny lies in our own hands — provided we understand this and do not let it go. Comprehending this, people however permit the environment to coerce and drag them on against their will. They renounce their self-sufficiency and, never relying on themselves, but on the environment alone, strengthen the ties linking them with it more and more. They expect that all the good and the evil of life will come from it, and depend least of all upon themselves. With such childish obedience, the fateful power of the external becomes irresistible. To engage in struggle with it seems insanity.

Alexander Herzen (1812–70),
Russian writer and revolutionary thinker.
'From the Other Shore', in *Selected Philosophical Works*.

FOREWORD

Harold D. Lasswell
Edward J. Phelps Professor of Law and Political
Science, New Haven, Connecticut, USA

F EW short treatises can be more timely than this exemplary sketch of the problem of corruption. Disproportionate emphasis has been put in recent years of the technological, scientific and economic dimensions of social change, with insufficient treatment of the many other value-institution features inseparable from the processes involved. Not the least of these neglected aspects is corruption, a complex and pervasive phenomenon to be differentiated from criminality, for example, and other closely connected but distinctive patterns of organized and unorganized behaviour.

Professor Alatas has deflated a great many hypotheses that have been put forward to account for some of the corruption that has so often appeared during the years of transition from a 'traditional' society. Intimately informed as a scholar and a participant of the details of many cultures, notably those in Southern and Eastern Asia, the author has, for instance, quietly challenged the supposed impact of the 'gift' as a traditional cultural practice whose predisposing effect has been to further a contemporary sub-culture of corruption. He has successfully dealt with one of the most commonly mentioned consequences that is often alleged to justify the policies of toleration on the part of those who influence official and private acquiescence in corrupt acts. Professor Alatas spells out with great lucidity the definitional distinctions and the kinds of historical and contemporary data that must be brought into the analysis before credence can be given to the suggestion.

This temperate, scholarly and acute analysis is a prologue to what I hope will be a new burst of scientific, scholarly and policy-oriented effort to bring our understanding of corruption to the level that has been attained in the study of some other social manifestations. The approach is eminently sound because it is thoroughly contextual. Professor Alatas makes it unmistakably clear that the phenomenon in question can only be grasped when it is explicitly related to the cultural setting where it appears and with which it continually interacts.

Only the most superficial mind could be satisfied with reflecting that the 'corrupt' like the 'poor' are always with us, and that nothing new can be learned by exploring the form and magnitude of corruption in any specific nation or locality. On the contrary, significant dimensions are only revealed when it is possible to identify the particular constellation of factors present in a given place at a definite time, and to ascertain their relative weight in stimulating or inhibiting corruption.

Without going further in underlining the importance of the present topic or its treatment, let me add my voice to those who will perceive in this discussion a fresh start in comprehending and contributing to the eventual control of one of the most recalcitrant characteristics of public and private life of yesterday or today anywhere in the community of man.

PREFACE

THE first published edition, comprising the first part of this book, was originally a paper submitted to the 27th World Congress of Orientalists, Ann Arbor, Michigan, USA, in August 1967. Only the abstract was published in its proceedings. However, eleven years earlier, my interest in writing on corruption had started as part of a general appraisal of the fundamental problems generated by colonialism.[1] A few years later, my contribution on corruption appeared in a Singapore daily.[2] Here I stressed amongst others that the integrity of an official must be considered as an absolute condition to qualify him for a job, for efficiency alone does not ensure against corruption; that the state should emphasize the moral factor in its education policy; that the state should consider religion as an ally in the fight against corruption; that sound social, political and economic planning be introduced.

The attempt to eliminate corruption must be based on taking into account human behaviour in its totality. Legal and administrative measures are not sufficient in themselves. Behind this, there must be a strong climate of opinion nurturing the sense of rectitude of such a strength that the ruling class becomes imbued by it. The absence of such a climate creates a situation prevailing in the developing societies, poignantly described by a Pakistani Minister of Justice and Parliamentary Affairs. Injustice and exploitation have prevailed for centuries. Touching on the tragic aspect of the prevailing system and society, he regretted that people had adopted false standards of distinction. Ill-gotten wealth had become the criterion of status and respectability. The younger generation in urban centres were worried about their future. Even legislation could not respond to the sense of anguish of human beings battered by such a system.[3]

The society alluded to above is one which has been invaded by what I have suggested should be called 'tidal corruption'. This is one in which the entire life is dominated by corruption. From top to bottom, government machinery is seriously infected by corruption. We are not talking of pockets of corruption here and there that exist in all societies. We are talking about the entire system of administration dominated by corruption entering into all levels of the decision-making process seriously affecting people's lives.[4] It is this kind of corruption, total corruption that grips a social order, that is the theme of this book.

Corruption is a highly complex phenomenon. It would not be possible to treat adequately its major features in a single book. Each scholar would have to make the selection he considers urgent and significant. Continuous research is necessary. In 1982–3, I was awarded a fellowship by the Woodrow Wilson International Center for Scholars, Washington DC. There I completed a book on a general theoretical and historical study of corruption in human society delving into areas not covered by the present book.[5] The two complement each other. There should be more books written on numerous other aspects of corruption. The material is inexhaustible. However, the need remains for a concise introductory treatment of the subject as presented in this book.

The present work covers a time span of thirty years. Chapter 1 was published as a booklet in Singapore, in 1968, under the title *The Sociology of Corruption*, by Donald Moore Press. Eighteen years later in 1986, together with Chapters 2 and 3, I wrote a continuation work under the title *The Problem of Corruption*, published by Times Books International, Singapore. Chapter 4 and the concluding chapter is a further extension. This book may thus be considered as a record of the evolution of the study of corruption in the author's mind for the last thirty years.

The purpose is not so much to document contemporary cases of corruption. It is to understand the phenomenon as broadly and as deeply as possible. The basic constituents of the phenomenon abide throughout history. The cruelty and rapacity of corruption, during the time of the Roman Empire, exhibited the same evil manifestation as that of the present time.

Gaius Verres (115–43 BC), the Roman governor of Sicily, prosecuted by Cicero, illustrated the unimaginable evil of corruption those in power were capable of. He committed extortion, plunder, bribery, rape, sexual exploitation of other men's wives, treachery, murder, looting works of art, selling public offices, money-lending at usurious rates, embezzling the wills of the deceased, and even extorted bribes from the parents and relatives of those condemned to death; for the manner of execution, a swift stroke of the axe or a slow painful death with torture. More than this, the manner of burial became also an issue of extortion; the corpses to be flung to the beasts or the parents to bury them.[6]

Extortion of parents anxious about the life of their children is practised today, in our present time. On 30 May 1989, a citizen of the then Soviet Russia, sent a telegram to the Minister of Health in Moscow, which was then forwarded to the Ukraine. His daughter, a 24-year-old mother, had a stomach operation and was released too soon. She was again operated along stitches which had not healed. According to the father who wrote the letter, she was then dying. In despair he wrote: 'The doctors here insist on big bribes, even though they know ahead of time that the patient is going to die.'[7] The only thing left for him and his relatives to do was to stage a hunger strike outside the hospital in Kharkov.

The evil motive to exploit the unfortunate in the most defenceless and vulnerable position is the same but the historical, social and cultural circumstances, as well as the type of activity involved, are different. In the phenomenology of corruption, new types of activity emerged but not the underlying motivation, scheming, enticing, extorting and controlling.

There is one thing in the nature of corruption which makes it different than other gainful activity. Corruption is never an end in itself. People are not corrupt for the sake of corruption. It is never considered as an end in itself, unlike gambling and profit-making activity. It is always a means to an end; wealth, power, influence, favours or control. Corruption apparently does not enter into the patho-psychological circuit of such a criminal behaviour as that of the kleptomaniac, who is obsessed with stealing for the sake of stealing, not for the value of the article, unlike the ordinary thief who goes for the value rather than the thrill of stealing. The corrupt does not express the act of corruption as a psychological relief compelled by an uncontrollable urge to do so. Such being the nature of corruption, it is a force which depends on sober planning and calculation with increasing sophistication and success, judged from its effect throughout the world.

The devastating effect of corruption throughout the world has gained more and more international attention. World bodies such as the United Nations, the Organization for Economic Cooperation and Development (OECD), the World Bank and numerous others have now recognized the gravity of the corruption problem. On the international crime situation, the Executive Director of Interpol, Raymond Kendall stressed the danger of worldwide corruption as the biggest obstacle in combating organized crime. Eastern European and Third World countries are particularly affected due to the systematic infiltration of their economies and political parties by corrupt elements.[8]

Finally I would like to revive the advice of Henry George, the well-known American author (1839–97) who fought hard against poverty, arising from his reaction to the book of the Duke of Argyll that explained how the feathers of a bird's wing were designed to give it power to fly and how the claw on the wing of a bat was intended for it to climb. Henry George reacted as follows: 'Will he let me ask him to look in the same way at the human beings around him? I will ask him to consider the little children growing up in city slums, toiling in mines, working in noisome rooms; the young girls chained to machinery all day or walking the streets by night; the women bending over forges in the Black Country or turned into beasts of burden in the Scottish Highlands; the men who all life long must spend life's energies in the effort to maintain life! He should consider them as he has considered the bat and the bird.'[9]

Human capabilities of body and mind, similar to the wings of the bird and the claws of the bat, had to be given the same appreciation and expectation of development as the biological endowments of the bird and the bat. Why should the Duke be born in possession of thousands of acres of land and others have no right to a single square inch?

Henry George invited the Duke of Argyll to appreciate the same truth in the endowment of Nature towards its creatures, in our social arrangement of living. It is good to be interested in knowledge but it should not justify neglect and human misery. Any branch of knowledge, particularly in the social sciences, cannot claim a moral status if it avoids dealing with human evil and the misery it generates.

Corruption is an all-encompassing evil because it is the common tool of all evil activities.

In the sixteenth century, Leonardo da Vinci (1452–1519), the great Renaissance figure, had drawn attention to the destruction of the environment and the presence of the uncouth and vulgar amongst the population. They did not merit the beautiful tools and contrivances of science. 'They deserve,' he said, 'rather nothing more than a sack in which to receive and excrete food, for they are but foodbags. They have nothing in common with the rest of the human race except their voices and their shapes; in everything else they are like beasts.'[10]

At this juncture of human history the reminder of Leonardo da Vinci is indeed timely. Scholars and others who study corruption should not be merely the foodbags of information and knowledge about corruption. They should not get excited by the wings of the bird and the claws of the bat without being moved by their misery in the struggle of existence. Henry George expressed the fundamental moral principle of the sciences that whatever we study should relate to the problem of human misery, the outcome of evil. No study of any segment of human life can be qualified as moral without reference to the phenomenon of corruption and injustice. A study of development excluding the decisive influence of corruption is a serious blunder which has only recently gained a corrective admission. More of this will be discussed in the concluding chapter.

I would like to thank the Woodrow Wilson International Center for Scholars, Washington DC for a substantial portion of Chapter 2 which was originally published by it as an occasional paper, delivered at its colloquium on 22 June 1983 during my fellowship there. I would also like to thank the Institute of Southeast Asian Studies, Singapore, for Chapter 4, 'The Problem of Corruption' which was previously published in its book *Management of Success*, Singapore, 1989.

The staff of the National University of Singapore Library and the National University of Malaysia Library had been most helpful in the preparation of this work. I would also like to express my deep regret that this time I was not able to benefit from the advice of the late Professor Harold D. Lasswell. Had he been alive his suggestions would have been of great benefit.

To my little grandson Emad, I owe a special debt of gratitude. Everytime I see his face, I wonder what kind of a world he would live in. Would it be free of corruption? Would he have to spend a great deal of inner energy to navigate his life through the waves of corruption which my generation and I had to do? Emad reminds me to keep on hoping and trying. For this I thank him.

SYED HUSSEIN ALATAS
November 1998

Endnotes

1. Syed Hussein Alatas, 'Some Fundamental Problems of Colonialism', *Eastern World*, London, November 1956.

2. Syed Hussein Alatas, 'The Effects of Corruption', *Singapore Tiger Standard*, Singapore, 28 February 1957.

3. *The Pakistan Times Overseas Weekly*, Lahore, 17 August 1986. Iqbal Ahmed Khan in a speech at the launching ceremony of an Urdu book by Zahid Hassan Chughtai.

4. See Appendix D, *The Asian Wall Street Journal*, Hong Kong, 25 February 1981.

5. Syed Hussein Alatas, *Corruption: Its Nature, Causes and Functions*, Gower Publishing Company, Aldershot, England, Brookfield, USA, 1990.

6. Cicero, *The Verrine Orations*, tr. L. H. G. Greenwood, Heinemann, London, 1935, vol. 1, 44, no. 116, p. 593.

7. Christopher Cerf and Marina Albee, *Small Fires*, Summit Books, New York, 1990, pp. 157–8. This is a collection of letter 1987–90, from the Soviet people to *Ogonyok magazine*.

8. *Transperency International News Letter*, Berlin, March 1997, p. 7.

9. Henry George, 'The Reduction to Iniquity', Nineteenth Century, July 1884, London, in Michael Goodwin, *Nineteenth Century Opinion*, Penguin Books, London, 1951, p. 61.

10. Leonardo da Vinci, *Philosophical Diary*, tr. Wade Baskin, Philosophical Library, New York, 1959, p. 71.

Chapter 1

THE SOCIOLOGY OF
CORRUPTION

ANYONE attempting a sociological analysis of corruption will eventually be confronted by a methodological problem. Accepted and generally applied methods of social research such as the interview, the questionnaire and statistical analysis cannot be applied here as long as corruption is considered as a shady transaction. The most that a sociologist can do is to observe the phenomenon and its effects and to gather as much confidential information as possible. Even public disclosures of corruption, such as those accompanying a fallen regime, do not reveal as much as there is to be revealed.

The sociologist studying the phenomenon of corruption has to be fully conversant with the history, the culture, the language and the circumstances of at least one rich and complex instance from which he can derive his data and test his theories. Without background knowledge, it is hardly possible to offer any fruitful insight beyond that which is obvious. Similarly, without a continuous sustained observation of the phenomenon over a long period, it is almost impossible to test the validity of certain generalizations on the nature and function of corruption.

A number of scholars who have treated the subject in some professional journals have done so as a sideline of their main interests. They did not keep a close watch on the phenomenon within a given country, selected as the concrete case, over a period of about ten or twenty years. The full cycle of corruption requires time to develop before its manifold ramifications can be observed. More than twenty years ago, Indonesia was already bogged down by corruption at all levels. It was firmly entrenched and received tacit protection from those in power, even though there was some public agitation against it. After the unsuccessful 30 September 1965 Communist attempt to seize power, followed by the rise of Generals Suharto and Nasution to leadership against the Communist–Sukarno united front, there was greater public agitation against corruption.

A new manifestation in the history of corruption in Indonesia was exposed in 1967, that is the role of banks in the intensification of corruption. Twenty years before this was hardly heard of. What did exist was the corruption of bank officials in the form of commissions (bribery) for loans obtained from banks, but with sufficient security. The new manifestation was the active participation of directors of some banks in organizing an illegal banking ring. Their banks issued large loans to clients without sufficient security. On 29 August 1967, fifteen banks were suspended and prohibited from clearing their cheques until investigation was completed. One of them was a bank for the armed forces. It was reported on 28 August 1967, that 39,000 dubious cheques from just three banks were being investigated. One army officer was alleged to have embezzled Rp120 million with the co-operation of a bank. It was subsequently claimed by the bank authorities that only Rp70 million was involved while the other Rp50 million was recovered. The officer involved escaped to Holland via Penang.[1]

These banks worked through unofficial agents whose function was to settle the deal with the party in need of the credit. When a credit, say of Rp10 million, was needed, the borrower had not only to pay a higher rate of interest (the official rate plus the illegal rate for the director, sometimes totalling up to 20 per cent) but also a 10 per cent down payment as soon as the amount was drawn from the bank. In a loan of ten million, one million was immediately deducted as a bribe for the director. As this practice developed, the bank as a whole had to draw overdraft from the central bank since more and more credit was given in this way.[2] Not only the banks, but other official or private institutions developed what General Nasution called 'dualism' in his written address to the Conference of Muslim Students in North

Sumatra on 26 August 1967. In it, he pointed out that after twenty-two years of independence, the Indonesian nation had not succeeded in establishing a just and prosperous society. General Nasution feared that corruption would turn out to be the national cancer unless it was mentally and administratively uprooted. He noted the dualism in the budgeting of some official institutions engendered by certain social and operational needs, as one of the sources of corruption.[3]

In a corrupt society, dualism in the activity of the state institutions is most pronounced. In every instance there is the official and the unofficial procedure. Tax assessors visit the home and offer to reduce assessment on remuneration. Admission to the university can be procured through the back door. Licences and permits can be obtained likewise. This dualism exists in almost every official activity there.

The association of corruption and crime is a well-known phenomenon. But the forms of this association vary according to the degree of corruption. As corruption develops in intensity these forms multiply. Thus on 11 August 1967, a Jakarta paper reported the arrest of seventeen people, some of them from the Indonesian Armed Forces, who organized a syndicate to sell or rent out firearms to those who needed them for private, often criminal purposes. The *modus operandus* was as follows: A soldier was ordered by his superior officer to perform a certain task, requiring a rifle, outside Jakarta. He was given between Rp6,000 and Rp15,000 as an allowance for a month. Whether the soldier in fact carried out the job, nobody bothered to ascertain. The rifle was then sold for Rp11,000, or rented out for a substantial fee. Every month the order was repeated. The proceeds from the sale of the rifle and the misappropriated monthly allowance were then divided. A recent raid by the authorities on a house at Djatipetamburan, Jakarta, recovered eleven rifles and ten blank orders sheets.[4]

Large-scale smuggling of tin from Banka involving some members of the Armed Forces was another instance of the association of corruption and crime. The Brigadier General who ordered the arrest of six army personnel, claimed that only one out of every ten shipments of tin per night could be traced. He was certain that the smuggling ring included military and civil authorities.[5] On 7 September 1967, a shipment of Indonesian tin worth RM20,000 was confiscated at

Tanjong Piai. This incident also involved members of the Armed Forces.[6]

Though we could acquire some occasional quantitative data on corruption, these would be by no means sufficient to justify any attempt to assess the cost of corruption. The known cases of corruption are only an insignificant part of this activity. The attempt to assess the cost of corruption and to set up a typology thereof, such as that expressed by Nye, is entirely fruitless in the absence of statistical data. It could not go beyond generalizations which are already obvious.[7] On the other hand, research into the phenomenology and typology of corruption, as well as its function as influenced by prevailing circumstances in a country enveloped by corruption, may yet help us to increase our understanding and explanation of the phenomenon.

Absence of sufficient quantitative data does not mean that there is nothing else to be examined. The effects of developed corruption are very obvious. In the case of Indonesia, nobody from any political party or any social or administrative group has ever denied the prevalence of corruption. The effects are too glaring to hide. The aim of the first chapter of this book is not a descriptive study of corruption in any particular area, but a theoretical exploration of the phenomenon, supported by available contemporary data on corruption.

This book does not aspire to give a specific concrete solution to the problem that could be adopted in a particular country. The prevention of corruption as discussed here refers to general conditions. A solution meant for any particular country has to be preceded by intensive case study with the co-operation of the government concerned. It has to go into details pertaining to the administrative, economic, political, social, cultural, philosophical and ethical aspects of corruption as found in the particular country under study.

Many problems have repeated themselves throughout history. The great Chinese reformer, Wang An Shih (AD 1021–86) in his attempt to eliminate corruption was impressed by the two ever-recurrent sources of corruption, bad laws and bad men. As he put it, 'But what I wish particularly now to emphasize is that history proves it to be impossible to secure proper government by merely relying on the power of the law to control officials when the latter are not the right men for their job.

4

It is equally futile to expect efficient government if, having the right men in their proper positions, you hedge them about by a multitude of minute and harassing prohibitions.'[8] His views on the dynamics and pathology of administration are extremely instructive, and contain much that is relevant to current interest in the problem. He classified human beings into two groups, the morally mediocre and the morally high. Changes of fortune did not affect the latter. The danger comes when the moral mediocrities gained control of government. Their action might then release all sorts of corrupt forces throughout the hierarchy.

Wang An Shih was no armchair theoretician. He was a very active public figure who once rose to the highest ministerial office of China, and who had a sound diagnosis of corruption. In the last analysis the two absolute prerequisites against corruption, he believed, were power-holders of high moral calibre, and rational and efficient laws. Neither could function without the other. The one conditioned the other. Both had to be present for any effort to be successful. The aim of modern governments for efficiency and rational goals is evident in Wang An Shih's approach. The Indonesian situation at that time led many of the country's serious-minded patriots to revive the issues. The problems confronted by Wang An Shih in eleventh-century China have again emerged under a new guise in contemporary Indonesia and many other Asian countries.

Amongst the Islamic scholars, Abdul Rahman Ibn Khaldun (AD 1332–1406) should be especially mentioned. He is well known not only as the discoverer of scientific history and sociology, but also as a student of corruption. Like Wang An Shih, he was no armchair theoretician. He was an active public figure who rose several times to high office, suffered imprisonment and various changes of fortune. During his appointment as a judge he tried to eliminate corruption and bribery but failed, and was dismissed from office. Ibn Khaldun attempted to explain the causes of corruption, and also why at certain times reformers had failed, and at other times they had succeeded. His insight into the matter is interesting. He considered the root cause of corruption to be the passion for luxurious living within the ruling group. It was to meet the cost of luxurious living that the ruling group resorted to corrupt

5

dealings. The other causes were further effects generative of further corruption.[9] They were the chain reactions released by corruption. The corruption of the ruling group brought about economic difficulties, and these difficulties in turn induced further corruption.

Between the old and the present studies of corruption in Asia, there has not been any continuity in the development of theory and analysis. Furthermore, the sociology of corruption in general has received relatively little attention from social scientists.

In most instances, reference to corruption is made in connection with other subjects, such as crime or public administration. Many works referring to corruption do not attempt a conceptual and causal analysis. Neither do they attempt to classify the types and degrees of corruption.[10] A theoretical enquiry into the roots and function of corruption as attempted by Rogow and Lasswell is not a common phenomenon.[11] Neither is Wertheim's discussion on the sociological aspects of corruption in Southeast Asia.[12]

THE NATURE OF CORRUPTION

Before we go any further, we should clarify the term 'corruption'. As Wertheim puts it, 'According to the common usage of the term "corruption" of officials, we call corrupt a public servant who accepts gifts bestowed by a private person with the object of inducing him to give special consideration to the interests of the donor. Sometimes also the act of offering such gifts or other tempting favours is implied in the concept. Extortion, i.e. demanding of such gifts or favours in the execution of public duties, too, may be regarded as "corruption". Indeed, the term is sometimes applied to officials who use the public funds they administer for their own benefit; who, in other words, are guilty of embezzlement at the expense of a public body.'[13]

Another phenomenon which can be described as corruption is the appointment of relatives, friends or political associates to public offices regardless of their merits and the consequences on the public weal. For the present purpose we shall call this nepotism.

We have thus three types of phenomena contained in the term corruption: bribery, extortion, and nepotism. They are not completely identical, but can be classified under one heading. Essentially there is a common thread running through these three types of phenomena—the subordination of public interests to private aims involving a violation of the norms of duty and welfare, accompanied by secrecy, betrayal, deception and a callous disregard for any consequence suffered by the public.

In the interests of analysis we have to differentiate further between corruption and criminal behaviour, and between corruption and maladministration or mismanagement of affairs, the effects of which are also not in the public interest.[14] But first let us enumerate the characteristics of corruption, and thereafter distinguish it from criminal behaviour not usually classified as corruption, and from maladministration or mismanagement of which many effects are the same as those of corruption.

The characteristics of corruption are as follows: (a) Corruption always involves more than one person. This need not be the case with stealing, for instance, or embezzlement. The lone operator in corruption is virtually non-existent, and such cases usually fall under fraud. One instance is making a false declaration of travelling expenditure or hotel bills. But even here there is often a silent understanding between officials who practise such fraud to let the situation prevail.[15] (b) Corruption on the whole involves secrecy, except where it has become so rampant and so deeply rooted that some powerful individuals or those under their protection would not bother to hide their activity. But nevertheless, even here the corrupt motive is kept secret. (c) Corruption involves an element of mutual obligation and mutual benefit. The obligation or benefit need not always be pecuniary. (d) Those who practise corrupt methods usually attempt to camouflage their activities by resorting to some form of lawful justification. They avoid any open clash with the law. (e) Those who are involved in corruption are those who want definite decisions and those who are able to influence those decisions. (f) Any act of corruption involves deception, usually of the public body or society at large.[16] (g) Any form of corruption is a betrayal of trust. (h) Any form of corruption involves a contradictory dual function of those who are committing the act. When an official is bribed to issue a business licence by the party who offers a 'gift', the act of issuing the licence is a function of both his office and his self-interest. He acts in a dual contradictory function. The same may be said of the party offering the bribe. Applying and receiving the licence is a function of his lawful business interest, but resorting to bribery is not. (i) A corrupt act violates the norms of duty and responsibility within the civic order. It is based on the deliberate intent of subordinating common interest to specific interest.[17]

The above list of characteristics of corruption could be extended. It is by no means exhaustive, but it is sufficient to function as a set of criteria by which the phenomenon of corruption can be classified. For an act to be classified as corrupt it has to contain all the above characteristics. These characteristics are drawn up through enumerative induction. During the past forty years, in which I have witnessed or heard of acts of corruption too numerous in form and content to recount, I have not come across a single instance where these traits are absent. The only possible exception is where corruption is difficult to distinguish from criminal extortion, where the party who bribes is compelled to do so, grudgingly and resentfully, and where the bribery is not considered as a necessary outlay for future gain. In such cases the victims kept no secrecy.

At this juncture, the description of corruption is not meant to be evaluative. The terms 'betrayal', 'deception' and 'unlawful', are used here in a neutral sense, without judging whether the act as such is good or bad for the particular society, and here again, good or bad as conceived by the society concerned. We shall deal with this later, in connection with the role and effects of corruption in the underdeveloped countries of Asia and Africa.

It is generally admitted that corruption is an age-old problem and that all human societies, except the very primitive, are, to some extent, in varying degrees, affected by corruption. Depending on the degree of corruption, and a set of other conditions, it has been successfully pointed out that the viability and development of a political, social, cultural or economic order, need not necessarily be stultified or thwarted by the mere presence of corruption. Some observers go further and claim that in some instances corruption has helped to promote economic development and efficiency.[18]

It has also been suggested that bureaucratic corruption today in underdeveloped countries is either encouraged by or merely continuous with the traditional offering of gifts to those in office or holding certain powers.[19] A lag in administrative adjustment in some areas and the persistence of earlier outlooks had contributed to the problem of corruption. As Wertheim described it with reference to Indonesia, 'First of all we have to take into account that the post-war forms of so-called corruption still frequently conceal relics of the traditional social structure. Village headmen for example are still unpaid, so that they have to maintain themselves by partly legal, partly illegal levies on the population. The patrimonial–bureaucratic substructure still influences all other sections of society, while traditional family ties continue to clash with modern concepts of morality in public affairs. Even as late as 1957 in several public services in Western Sumatra, it could be observed that all the personnel in one particular office belonged to a single family group, that of the office chief.'[20]

A discussion of corruption may be divided into three problem areas: (a) the function of corruption, (b) the causes of corruption, and (c) the ways and means of eliminating or restraining the influence of corruption. So far no trend encouraging and promoting corruption as an ideal has emerged among social scientists. Even those who claimed to see some positive aspects of corruption have not recommended it for development but only tolerated it. It is apparent that there can be no sufficiently fruitful insight into the subject if these three problem areas are not covered at the same time in an analysis, at least at this present stage of enquiry where there is still a lack of conceptual differentiation and methodological caution. The underlying methodological assumptions on social causation, on historical continuity, on the emergence of new cultural values, on the identification and interpretation of social phenomena have to be brought into the area of discourse.

THE FUNCTIONS OF CORRUPTION

It will shortly be apparent that suggestions on the causes and function of corruption in underdeveloped countries have suffered from serious methodological shortcomings. The best instance at hand is the claim that corruption has some positive contribution to make for the progress of underdeveloped areas. The first objection we may raise against Weiner and Spiro, and many others dealing with the problem is that they did not first meaningfully define and differentiate substantially the concept of corruption into the three major types, and then assess its function in terms of each of these. Extortion, nepotism and bribery each possess a distinct dynamics and phenomenology. Their effects and functions with reference to development differ according to the context of a country's situation and cultural background. If we desire to appraise the functions of corruption in a particular context, we will have to assess each of the three separately.

Many observers like Weiner and Spiro, to mention only two, generalize about the function of corruption in a particular country like India, or a particular region such as those in the underdeveloped areas, on data derived from a particular type of corruption. It has been suggested by Weiner that by bribing the officials the businessmen could get things done which otherwise would have taken a long time, owing to innumerable regulations. 'Indeed, the *bakshish* system is not as disruptive as might first appear. It lends to the administrative system discretion and flexibility (which admittedly are provided by other means in other systems) without which many businessmen would find it difficult to function.'[21] Weiner noted the view of many businessmen that if government were to impose all the regulations, business and economic growth would come to a grinding halt. He appeared to endorse this view when he said, 'On the other hand, we have tried to suggest in our study that efforts to influence local administration, even through widespread corruption, are not wholly detrimental to political, and perhaps even to economic, development.'[22]

As a statement of fact limited to the type of corruption concerned, there is no disagreement with Weiner. As a matter of fact, people living in such an area are fully aware of the instrumental function of

10

corruption for specific purposes. Some of them have done a bit of theorizing. In a discussion with a businessman in Jakarta several years ago, I was made aware of a significant classification of corruption suggested to me by this businessman. This gentleman, who was then active in business, and who constructed and sold houses and engaged in internal trade, was an honest and philanthropic man. He classified two forms of corruption, but had been involved with only one of these. He said that in cases in which he had been involved, he was merely paying for his right. The instances he cited were: obtaining approval for certain construction programmes, and exit permit to go abroad, and a host of other approvals required by regulations which are non-competitive but merely routine in nature. In these instances he claimed that he was merely buying his rights; in other words, he allowed himself to be extorted. The government officials forced him to offer bribes, otherwise, his business would come to a grinding halt.

It would be different, he suggested, if he were to deprive other people of their rights. For instance, he could attempt to pay a heavy bribe to get an occupation permit for a house, thereby depriving another more entitled to it by right. Or he could pay to buy a job for an undeserving relative, or buy a licence for a pump station. This type of corruption he considered wrong and unethical.[23] Whatever his views were on the subject, the interesting point for us is his classification of corruption into types. He clearly brought forward the extortive type of corruption, and it is this type of corruption which Weiner, Spiro and some others consider as functional within the actual set-up in underdeveloped countries.

Without denying the fact that such a type of corruption does act as a promoter of efficiency in this particular context, the fact is not of great interest for planning or research, for the simple reason that it belongs to that category of findings which is obvious. It is a known fact that the expansion and sophistication of criminal activity has, in several instances, increased the efficiency of the police, just as it is a fact that the miseries suffered by countless victims of cancer have helped cancer research. Such a viewpoint is not of much use since almost everything happening under the sun can be said to be positive in some way. We are more interested in the total context, the context of society which has made graft 'the oil that makes the administrative machinery operate quickly'. It is when we consider graft in the total context that we get a different picture of the function of extortive corruption. The following examples can be observed by anyone who has the time and patience to look out for the effects of extortive corruption:

(a) The infinite frequency of graft transactions involving countless millions of dollars and hundreds of thousands of business decisions in the underdeveloped countries becomes a burden to the public, since the cost of graft is eventually passed on to the consumer. Where there is no effective price control, manufacturers and businessmen always attempt to transfer the burden of legal taxation to consumers. The same holds true of graft, which is a kind of illegal taxation.

(b) Though graft helps to promote efficiency in particular cases, it tends to lower the efficiency of the civil service as a whole. In an office or a department riddled with corruption, the efficiency norms of the bureaucracy has always to be subordinated to the norms of the graft ring. Efficient and honest civil servants have been known to be transferred or blocked from promotion if their presence or promotion affects the interest of the ring.

(c) In actual practice, extortive corruption is a phenomenon which tends to spread rapidly, bringing along with it negligence and inefficiency. It is never restricted to one form. The habit of doing something illegal and subversive becomes transferred to wider and wider circles, unless effectively restrained. The type of bribery alleged to promote efficiency has the tendency to develop and extend the habit in areas where it is difficult to promote efficiency.

(d) Corruption undermines respect for the constituted authority. This in turn leads to innumerable kinds of serious problems. It tends to deprive a government of public support, and alienates public devotion to government's aims.

Furthermore, such bribery is not always effective. Within the context of corrupt relationships, there is also competition based on corruption norms. Those who pay most are not always the ones who succeed. The trustworthiness of the bribe-giver, the extra favours he could offer, like providing women, or facilities for holidays, or some kind of assistance, may determine the receptiveness of the officials. We have seen that conclusions derived from one type of corruption cannot be made the basis of a generalization on corruption in general. It is also apparent that in actual practice, it is difficult to suggest the effect of extortion on efficiency as isolated from its effect on other types of corruption and the total context.

There is a further aspect of the problem. When extortive corruption has become widespread within an administration, it is usually the result of previous conditions of corruption. In our analysis of the problem of corruption, we should have a theory of its dynamics and developmental stages. So far no such theory has been presented.

A methodological shortcoming in a study on corruption is evidenced in Colin Leys's treatment of the problem. 'The Uganda Minister of Information,' he says, 'was much criticized for giving a lucrative and unusual monopoly of television set sales to an American contractor, in return for building a transmission station at cut rates: even had corruption been involved, the policy did produce a television station much more quickly and cheaply than the policy adopted in neighbouring Kenya.'[24]

The point to be examined in this case is the place of the television station in the hierarchy of priorities, both in terms of the objective national conditions as well as government policy. If it is in terms of government policy, we should enquire whether that policy which places the television station as of a definite priority, is not actuated by corrupt motives. Corruption is not restricted to the acts of specific decisions. It is a process involving attitude build-up, deliberate planning, historical antecedents, social mobility, group affiliation, and other sociological factors.[25] Therefore we have to examine the context as a whole. In the case of the television station we must look at the wider framework of government policy, and assess whether the group responsible for this policy is free from corruptive motivation in constructing and implementing their hierarchy of priorities.

Leys claims that not all kinds of inequality promoted by

corruption are beneficial from the point of view of development. But he challenges the assumption that they are invariably bad.[26] The concepts 'beneficial' and 'bad' are not defined by Leys. Neither is the concept of development. We do not wish to split hairs here and insist that he write a treatise on these points. But Leys himself insists on the description, measurement, analysis and explanation of corruption, and attacks what he considers to be the moralist concept of corruption. In his attempt at a critical analysis of this concept, he appears to favour a relativistic position, leaving the group and society concerned to define it.[27]

However, even this position demands a classifying set of criteria to group the different phenomena of corruption under various headings. For example, there are different conceptions of the abnormal personality cherished by different peoples and cultures. Here a certain degree of relativistic explanation is justified. However, we are not justified in eliminating altogether the objective universal criteria of abnormality employed by psychology. A paranoiac is a paranoiac whether he is the president of a modern state or the chief of a primitive tribe. It is true that a society's response to the afflicted person, and the interpretation of its function and implication differ, but the underlying phenomena, for purposes of scientific clarification and classification, do not.

The conceptualization of corruption suggested at the beginning of this book aims at universality, like any concept of science seeking general classification. The difficulty of isolating some incidents of corruption is a practical problem, not a theoretical one. We may illustrate this by another instance from Leys's article. In Kampala, Uganda, in August 1963, the City Council granted a petrol station site to a member of the majority party who offered the lowest price, £4,000, the highest bid being £11,000. It was subsequently alleged, and later denied, that the successful bidder later resold the plot to an oil company at a profit of £8,000. In the subsequent debate in the City Council, the majority party defended its decision with the argument that the Council was not obliged to accept the highest offer, and that the Council preferred to give a 'stake' in the city to a poor man rather than to a rich one.

The opposition maintained that the decision was swayed by

political favouritism, rather than the man's poverty. Even should helping the poor be the motive, the loss of a great amount of public revenue was too high a price to pay. They further maintained that in this case the official policy should have been to accept the highest bid, unless public interest, not present in this case, dictated otherwise. Leys cited this instance to illustrate his point that the nature of official rule has to be clarified before assessing whether or not an act is corrupt. In cases like this, it may be difficult to pass judgement from a distance, but the intent of the act is the essential qualifying factor. The problem we are facing here is a practical one.

Theoretically speaking we may adopt the following formulation: 'Not all acts which benefit the office-holder at the expense of the people are corrupt, else the term would include all taxation by an absolute monarch to provide accustomed luxuries for his family and court, all fees and dues paid by serfs to their feudal lords, all sacrifices and gifts given to the priestly class in theocracies. Acts illegal in themselves and calculated to benefit the office-holders are obviously corrupt. But neither the question of formal legality nor that of the sufferance of the act by the mass of people is of the essence of the concept. Where the best opinion and political morality of the time, examining the intent and setting of an act, judge it to represent a sacrifice of public for private benefit, it must be held corrupt.'[28]

Not only in the case of corruption, but also in that of other social phenomena, recourse to concrete analysis is necessary in order to identify the nature of such phenomena. Some problems can be answered only through direct contact with the concrete data, and through concrete contextual analysis. In the case of the example cited above, actual participation, membership of the group, and adequate background knowledge of the situation as well as the personalities of those involved will enable us to judge whether an act is corrupt.

Those who suggest the positive function of corruption in underdeveloped areas, apart from ignoring certain dimensions in contextual analysis, have also been guilty of a bias in their selection of data.

Here are some descriptions of corruption in certain countries in Latin America, which can also be applied to some Asian countries I

15

know from experience. These data are often ignored or missed by those who suggest some positive function of corruption. People fear the police and their extortions, of which the most common form is the imposition of fines for fictitious offences, the money going to the policemen. In some countries, the ordinary people regard the police as extortioners or uniformed bandits. In most countries the clerks have to be bribed to deal with the innumerable formalities, failing which, they attend to the matter with deliberate delay or not at all. Customs inspectors derive most of their income from bribes. In a particular Latin American country they damage or delay goods of people who do not offer a bribe. Furthermore, there is the distribution of contracts to those who will reserve a cut for the ruling cliques. It was in this way that two Latin American presidents had directly appropriated US$700 million and US$400 million respectively. One deceased dictator had amassed an amount exceeding US$1,000 million.[29]

During the years following the terrible earthquake of May 1960, Chile received US$120 million from the United States as aid for the victims. By October 1961, out of 40,000 homeless only 3,000 were rehoused 'which would make it appear that it costs many thousand dollars to build a peasant's hut'.[30] Blankets, foodstuff and other materials sent to Peru for the victims of earthquakes and floods found their way into the shops of Lima and elsewhere.

When the total effect of corruption on afflicted societies, whether in the economic, administrative, political or judicial realms is considered, no stretch of sociological imagination could ever succeed in suggesting that it has some positive function in development, except in the development of exploitation, inequality, and moral and legal disorder. I will here cite Andreski's conclusion on the nature of corruption: 'The losses caused by corruption far exceed the sum of individual profits derived from it, because graft distorts the whole economy. Important decisions are determined by ulterior and anti-social motives regardless of the consequences to the community. When a useless factory is built in an impossible place simply because the former owner bribed the officials into buying it for an exorbitant price, then the cost to the community must far exceed the profits of the manipulators. An administrative machine permeated by graft does not respond to direction, so that even a most enlightened cabinet or president can achieve nothing, and his instructions are perverted in execution. The network of collusion is so thick that an honest president, even one as energetic as Cardenas, gropes as in a fog. Every bureaucratic machine suffers to some extent from an antipathy towards initiative and originality, from sycophancy and from the preferment of intriguers and yes-men. But when graft is added to these disorders, the machine ejects all the incurably honest men, selects for promotion the most ruthless and astute rogues, and compels the rest to follow their example.'[31]

Those who suggested some positive function of corruption did not link their analysis with the different stages of corruption, which is essential to the validity of their generalizations or suggestions. When we declare that corruption has some positive function, what stage of corruption do we have in mind?

THREE STAGES OF CORRUPTION

Broadly speaking, we may divide corruption into the following three stages:

(a) The stage at which corruption is relatively restricted without affecting a wide area of social life. In this stage we can accomplish without hindrance and extortion almost all our dealings with the government in most of our routine affairs. Rights and regulations are implemented without public suffering. Almost everything the public requires from the government can be obtained without recourse to graft or nepotism. At this stage corruption is restricted to a section of the upper circle in government and in big business.

(b) The second stage is where corruption has become rampant and all pervading. There is hardly anything anyone can do without graft. I shall illustrate this with the case of a Southeast Asian country which has been literally ruined by corruption. I had the good fortune to observe this directly having spent several years in the country through all the different periods of political change, the colonial rule, the Japanese occupation, and the independence.

17

From the time of the Japanese occupation up to the present day, more than fifty years have elapsed. During this period corruption has steadily increased. Twenty years ago, when I was in the capital of this country, there was hardly anything one could do without either graft or influential connection.

Tickets for air and rail travel were sold on the black market. A certain number of train tickets were sold regularly but the rest went to the black market. Bookings on local air flights were always full, but to the amazement of those who bought black-market tickets, there were often a number of empty seats on a plane. The telephone system was not automatic, and the operator had to be bribed. The postman had to be given a monthly *bakshish*. The office boy had to be tipped in advance to deliver a letter to his boss. The stamp counter at the post office claimed never to have small change as prices of small commodities were numerically big. One could not pass a driving test without rewarding the police examiner. Thousands of households, including the one in which I stayed, had to pay protection money to certain secret societies in order to buy security from their attack and protection from attack by rival groups. The police, however, were not concerned. The fire brigade did not always respond to an emergency. The garbage collector would leave the rubbish alone if he was not properly tipped. Even colleagues in the same department had to resort to bribery. Thus in the foreign ministry the officer in charge of accommodating returning members of the diplomatic staff to the home office expected bribes from less powerful colleagues.

Some time ago I asked a businessman, whom I have known for forty years, whether there was still anything left in that city's administration which could be achieved without bribery. His reply was: only fetching a registered letter from the post office! Between the capital and a certain town at the foot of a mountain, the journey took one and a half to two hours under normal pre-war road conditions. Some years later it took approximately four hours. The road had deteriorated through negligence and corruption, and although this country produces tar, the tar was sold on the black market. Many civil servants who had no

18

opportunity to extort, or who did not want to, as well as those that did, worked in more than one place to earn extra money. They left their offices before time to work elsewhere. I know a gentleman who for at least twelve years had worked in three places a day: in the morning, at a ministry, in the afternoon, in an embassy, and in the evening, in his own firm. Academicians lecture in several institutions. At one time, in one of the country's leading universities, one professor lectured on between ten and twelve different subjects in order to earn extra money.[32] The general economic chaos, the degraded state of the administration, the loss of authority, the disrespect for the administration, and the political disorder, have not only been pointed out by observers, but confirmed by the government and political leaders, and by almost everyone from that country.

(c) The third stage of corruption is the most interesting, and at times most difficult to notice. This is when corruption becomes self-destructive, having destroyed the fabric of society. To further our theory of the dynamics of corruption, we must here include its interplay with other factors. Corruption alone is not responsible for its destructive effects. We must also include here the cause and effect relationship of corruption. Corruption stimulates further development of greater corruption, and this further degree in turn causes an even greater increase in corruption. When extortion becomes widespread in the civil service, and is used by policemen on the beat, the clerk at the counter, and the nurse at the hospital, it is usually the effect of previous corruption at a higher level. For a country's condition to generate widespread corruption amongst the civil service, it requires that a preceding state of corruption be present and responsible for that condition. A theory of corruption has to include this initial condition.

Usually the succession from the stage of restricted corruption to the stage of widespread and deep-rooted corruption starts with the group which is least hampered by economic difficulties affecting their means of subsistence. This is the group of high officials and well-to-do businessmen. When corruption in this circle has gone on for some time, society will then feel the effect. The state revenue declines out of proportion to the volume of trade and taxable sources. The currency declines in value, and prices go up. When this happens, the lower levels of government officials take recourse to corruption in an effort to maintain their livelihood. But this general economic difficulty is generated by the corruption of the economically higher classes. There are many interesting variables here, which in their turn determine whether the corruption of the upper and influential classes will generate conditions for general corruption. Those who suggest some positive function in corruption base their analysis on this stage of corruption, and that is done only within the area of extortive corruption. They do not proceed to the next stage, which is when corruption becomes destructive not only of society, but, also of those practising it. There are a few countries in the underdeveloped areas going through this process. Some illustrative data from a country in Southeast Asia is given here.

Around the capital of this particular country to which I referred to earlier there are rail crossings across the main roads. The gate-keepers deliberately lower the gate pole much earlier than they are supposed to. Since the trains are often irregular, especially the baggage mails, it is not possible for the public to know whether this is done deliberately. As a result of this, the traffic is halted long before it is necessary and the travellers, many of whom are truck drivers, spend their time consuming food and drink at nearby stalls along the roadside. The proceeds from these sales are then shared with the gatekeeper.[33] The effect this has made on business and general efficiency can be imagined. The slowing up of transportation, the increase in labour hours, and the disruption of timing schedules, affect general efficiency. In no way is this positive to development. The effect of this type of corruption is no doubt different from giving *bakshish* for a permit. But the fact that corruption is of various motivations and actions should be an integral part of the whole approach to corruption. A businessman who 'greases his way' to get a permit does not stop there. He will eventually bribe his way along to ensure that he secures other conditions necessary to him. He will see that the official concerned remains at his post, he will attempt to block a competitor. In this situation anything may happen, and the element of insecurity is increased.[34]

An author who sees some positive value in corruption, reasons as follows: 'Since the licences and favours available to the bureaucrats are in limited supply, they are allocated by competitive bidding among entrepreneurs. Because the payment of the highest bribes is one of the principal criteria for allocation, the ability to muster revenue, either from reserves or from current operations, is put at a premium. In the long run both of these sources are heavily dependent on efficiency in production. Hence, a tendency towards competition and efficiency is introduced into the system.'[35] This reasoning is characteristic of those who claim that corruption has some positive function in development. In this article of approximately 7,500 words, only a few lines are devoted to concrete instances. It appears to be deductive, like an exercise in geometry, using a set of axioms to establish the conclusions.

The facts in underdeveloped countries point in the opposite direction. The fittest who survives is not always the most efficient and competitive. With the protection given to national industry and the security obtained by graft, neither efficiency nor competitiveness improves.[36] Instead these firms and industries in, for instance, the Southeast Asian country mentioned earlier, become gigantic centres for indirect embezzlement. As the state becomes poorer and poorer, business concerns become richer and richer. I am not suggesting that indirect or direct corruption is always correlative with inefficiency. Efficient and successful firms practise indirect and direct corruption too, as well as practising commercial espionage and diplomacy. But the significant fact about their efficiency and achievement is not the corruption they practise but their ability to maintain an efficient, rational and methodical approach, strengthened by capital potential and sufficient experience.

They are successful in the field of competitive corruption because they are already successful in the field of growth and efficiency. Their successful bids for definite orders and status at particular moments by means of corruption may be attributed more to their already successful achievements rather than to their resort to corruption. Most of the efficient and successful firms in underdeveloped areas have been those of long standing and experience. The history of their efficiency has never been correlative with their level of corruption. Their success is often due to the fact that they become indispensable, and that they are difficult to beat in fair or unfair competition. The extent and number of bribes offered by their rivals are often not in the least a decisive factor in their success in competition.

An instance where corruption is irrelevant to success and efficiency is that of pioneer industries in Malaysia. The Pioneer Industries (Relief from Income Tax) Ordinance, introduced in 1958, provides income tax exemption for between two and five years, based on the amount of fixed capital invested. A company with less than RM100,000 (the rate of exchange then was RM3 to US$1) receives relief for two years, and an additional year if its capital investment is between RM100,000 and RM250,000, with a further two years if the investment is above RM250,000. In 1964, 107 companies were given pioneer status. The main condition to obtaining such status is that the industry has not been run on a commercial scale suitable to the economic requirements of the nation and that there is scope for its development. The total nominal capital was RM650,160,000. The paid amount was RM166,472,892 out of which RM53,965,786 was local capital.[37]

It is difficult to imagine that the establishment of 107 industries involving a paid-up total capital of RM166,472,892 which was fairly substantial at the time did not involve a certain amount of corruption.[38] But what is of interest to us is that here corruption is not relevant to the efficiency factor. The point at which corruption would have been most necessary would have been in the obtaining of pioneer status. Once this is achieved the management and planning factors are of crucial importance within the system. The initial corruption is not relevant to growth and development. Since the industry is granted pioneer status, given the other conditions, the need to depend on graft for government service is less than otherwise. Furthermore, competition with other local industries in the same line is virtually non-existent. If graft was present, it decreased rather than increased efficiency, for graft, in this context, was often directed to the avoidance of improvement of quality.[39]

It has also been suggested that corruption can act as a hedge against bad policy. 'Even when the government of an underdeveloped country is proceeding actively and intelligently to promote growth, there is no assurance that its policies are well-conceived to attain its goals. In effect, it may be taking a vigorous step in the wrong direction. Corruption can reduce the losses from such mistakes, for while the government is implementing one policy, the entrepreneurs, with their sabotage, are implementing another. Like all insurance, this involves a cost—if the government's policy is correct. On the other hand, like all insurance, it is sometimes very welcome.'[40]

As the above extract shows, the author qualifies the validity of his suggestion by 'may' and 'can'. To support his suggestion he cites the example of Argentina and Chile. But Argentina and Chile have been corruption-riddled countries, with deep historical roots in corruption. The sabotage of Peron's economic policies by graft from agricultural producers is alleged to have had beneficial effects on Argentina's capacity to import.[41] The sabotage of Peron's policies is not analysed within the context of an already developing corruption. 'Corruption, always rampant in Argentina, reached fabulous proportions under Peron, when large parts of the economy came under governmental control. According to serious estimates, Peron accumulated US$700 million in his personal accounts in foreign banks. The traffic in permits and appointments was enormous.'[42] To sabotage Peron's policy through graft and to succeed is analogous to gang warfare with the victor possibly being capable of doing less harm to the public. Within this context, of course, it is an advantage. The exact situation should be defined as a relatively honest but bungling government being sabotaged by graft, the success of which leads to public advantage. However, such a viewpoint has never been put forward. The argument in favour of corruption as a means of sabotaging bad policy is, in my opinion, without convincing foundation.

This is not to deny that, within an already corrupt political and historical context, differences in policy can have consequences which are positive or negative. There is still a gradation in the degree and effect of corruption. To return to the case of Peron and his fatal policy of instituting government monopoly on agricultural produce, fixing uneconomic prices, and simultaneously preventing the import of goods required to maintain productivity, his government did succeed in causing food scarcity in a country abundant in food. The aftermath of this policy is still felt in Argentina many years later. In the case of Argentina, like some other underdeveloped countries, it was a combination of administrative inefficiency, incompetent planning and corruption. In fact, the three are often found together. To what extent each contributes to the total crisis or developmental strain and stagnation, requires a special investigation which has never been undertaken.

Peron's regime, like that of his predecessors had some positive contributions to make. But corruption played a significant role in their downfall. The cult of personality was pushed by Peron to degrading extremes, repelling honest citizens and leading to the invasion of the civil service by incompetent and dishonest sycophants. 'In addition to dislocating the economy, his rule aggravated the corruption and inefficiency of the administration; it stimulated appetites whilst reducing the means of satisfying them.'[43] The point of interest to us here is Andreski's evaluation of Peron's rule. 'He has raised the self-respect of the workers, helped them to organize themselves, extended facilities for free education, introduced social insurance and other measures of public assistance. Had he not squandered money on arms and ostentation, had he been an efficient and honest administrator, he could have put Argentina among the prosperous and stable societies.'[44]

Many countries in Asia and Africa have had similar experiences, in the sense of a combination of corruption, inefficiency and bad planning. Improvement lies in the decrease of all these, as far as national development is concerned. A permissive attitude towards corruption would impede development, however unavoidable corruption may be within particular contexts of action.[45] The need to overcome bureaucratic hurdles and numerous regulations of the kind noted by Weiner, though genuine, does not plead for the positive function of corruption. It should rather be seen as the expansion of corruption, for to some extent, corruption contributes to the enormous increase of rules and delays, and ostentatious projects that would benefit the corrupt power-holders. We also have to bear in mind that the inability of an administration to perform efficiently, in the face of an increasing number of rules and regulations, is partly due to corruption, while the administrative lag in performance contributes to the corruption cited as instances by Weiner and others.

In many underdeveloped countries we can notice the simultaneous occurrence of three trends, i.e. expansion of the civil service, increase of rules and regulations, and decrease in reserve revenue. All three may be determined to a large extent by the need to implement development projects. But already at the earliest stages, before the projects are even conceived of and approved, corruption has emerged in a form which affects the revenue, with or without the prolific multiplication of rules. Whether there is expansion of government activity or not, corruption is there and it expands with governmental expansion. From whichever point of view we look at it, it does not contribute positively towards development, for a part of government funds is continuously drained for negative purposes. In the last analysis, the function of corruption is comparable to a disease; if well under control, harmless, if not deadly.[46]

THE CAUSES OF CORRUPTION

We may now turn our attention to the causes of corruption. It has been suggested that corruption has been brought about by the following factors: (a) The absence or weakness of leadership in key positions capable of inspiring and influencing conduct mitigating corruption. As the Chinese and Japanese proverb says, 'As the wind blows so bends the reed.' (b) The weakness of religious and ethical teachings. (c) Colonialism. An alien government does not awaken the necessary loyalty and devotion capable of inhibiting corruption. (d) Lack of education. (e) Poverty. (f) Absence of severe punitive measures. (g) Absence of environment conducive to anti-corrupt behaviour. (h) Structure of government. (i) Radical change. Whenever a value system is undergoing a radical change, corruption appears as a transitional malaise. (j) The state of society. Corruption in a bureaucracy reflects the total society.[47]

Although the above factors are the constituent elements in the occurrence of corruption, yet by themselves, these factors are not sufficient to explain the phenomenon. In his stimulating study of this problem, Braibanti has accumulated some concrete arguments against invoking them separately as an explanation of corruption. As he puts it, 'Their importance lies in the fact that they are but elements in a complicated matrix of causes, each of which are of varying importance, depending on spatial, temporal and circumstantial factors.'[48]

The idea of the personal influence of leaders concentrically radiating virtue like pebbles causing ripples to the edges when dropped into a pool of water, inclines towards a highly optimistic view of human nature. In a simple tribal society the influence radiating from the leaders may reach the followers directly, without involving a network of complex factors of transmission. 'But in large, complex organizations, the virtue of the leader is not enough. The pristine quality of the image of his virtue is too easily tarnished and even eroded by the complexity of his indirect relations with his subordinates.'[49] There are several historical instances of good leaders with bad governments, and bad governments with good leaders.

The other factors noted are, on examination, similarly inadequate. Here we shall restrict our discussion to one social factor alleged to have contributed to corruption. This is the suggestion that underdeveloped traditional societies contain the institution of the gift which easily shades into corruption.[50] That this may happen need not be denied. What can be refuted is the tenability of the claim that this practice is one of those significant determinants of corruption arising from within the traditional context. It has been suggested that nepotism is a form of family obligation. 'To resist bribery and not to resort to nepotism may very well constitute avoidance of the responsibilities of customary citizenship.'[51] It seems to me that this is a misinterpretation, as the transfer of traditional norms into a modern bureaucratic setting is here considered as a continuation of traditional behaviour. The misinterpretation lies in the fact that such behaviour is not considered as an abuse of traditional norms, with the area of action being a modern bureaucracy. To substantiate this with arguments we must first look at the forms of corruption.

The aspects that corruption can take on are probably unlimited. Apart from direct bribing, extortive on otherwise, the indirect approach is also interesting. The example given in protests against corruption and abuses by some Dutch civil servants around the turn of the century in Java give us some interesting illustrations. This form of indirect corruption is based on the ingenuity in giving a plausible reason for accepting bribes. Thus a junior European administrative official on being transferred to another post, would put up his belongings for auction, and in such auctions a pen might fetch 100 guilders. An inkstand was once purchased by the manager of an oil company for 510 guilders, a cigar-cutter for 350 guilders, purchased by the manager of a tobacco company, and a globe for 600 guilders purchased by a manager of another tobacco company.[52]

Japanese writers on Japanese development, writing in 1951–2, had noted some of the forms of corruption which were then current practice. Government officials well known to business and industry had no difficulty in finding attractive positions upon leaving government service.[53] Expensive banquets and receptions came to be regarded as an essential part of official procedure. Payrolls were padded as a means of raising entertainment funds. In government public works, 15 per cent of the total amount appropriated was said to have been spent on entertainment. There were five accepted ways of corrupting officials, i.e. to give them money, to allow them prestige, to give them drink, to give them food, and last but not least to provide them with lavish geisha entertainment. After World War II some new forms of corruption emerged. These included the sending of gifts or presents to officials upon their arrival or departure, and on occasions like the birth of a child; and at mahjong parties where officials were allowed to win large sums of money by those seeking favours.[54]

In Malaysia, Singapore and Brunei, these forms of corruption are still operative. There is yet another form, which is to bet on a game of golf and lose to a higher official. The official who wins such a bet does not commit any crime. We have also the example of the sale of second-hand cars. Thus a subordinate would buy his superior's car at a slightly higher price than that which he would have to pay in the open market, in return for assistance in obtaining promotion. Indirect embezzlement of government funds through commissions delivered through a supplier or purchaser, depending on the nature of the government transaction, is common. Another form of embezzlement is padding travelling expenses. Hotels and restaurants are willing to provide false bills. Perhaps the most subtle form of embezzlement is the practice of making inspection trips or other official trips, when that minister or official himself decides when and how often trips should be made. By these means, claims for travelling allowances can be ensured to flow in, conveniently increasing the income.

THE GIFT

An exposition of the forms of corruption suggests that corruption, like a parasitic plant, will creep around any suitable firmament serving its purpose, and of all the possible firmaments the institution of the gift is the most obvious. But this fact alone does not justify the conclusion that the gift is an indirect causal agent peculiar to the region in the growth of corruption in underdeveloped areas. The gift is a universal institution. It is prevalent in Western society as much as it is in other parts of the world. That there is no significant causal correlation between the gift and corruption is proved by the fact that the expansion and contraction of corruption has nothing to do with a similar occurrence in the field of gift behaviour. Furthermore, the indirect causal influence of a gift is multi-dimensional. It can turn people away from corruption, apart from attracting them to it. I will clarify this point later.

It is to be understood that here we are concerned with gifts offered in return for bureaucratic services. The following observation, an actual instance from Vietnam, serves our purpose: 'Although this is not the place to discuss the general problems of corruption of administrators, it is necessary to make a rather detailed analysis of this irregular element of the decision-making process. Before the arrival of the French, administration was set up so as to cost as little as possible and to keep intervention in the social life of the people to a minimum. This double principle is the result of the adoption of the idea of virtue as the basis of administrative action. In principle, the government demanded contributions from the people only to the extent that these contributions were necessary to the functioning of the administration. This contribution was first made on a voluntary basis each time a

28

citizen had occasion to ask for the services of a mandarin, but later became obligatory and uniform. Royal edicts regulated precisely the quality and quantity of gifts the communal or cantonal authorities were to make to the mandarin district chiefs on entering the administrative service, on New Year's Day, on being promoted to a higher rank, on presenting a request, etc. Similarly, gifts were presented by the mandarins themselves to their superiors, progressively up the hierarchy to the king. It should be noted that there was a certain reciprocity in this exchange of presents: on less frequent and more solemn occasions, the king himself sent gifts to the high-ranking mandarins, who did the same to their subordinates, and so on, down the ladder.'[55]

It is apparent that giving presents was part of traditional administration. But the phenomenon differed sharply from corruption. (a) It was not committed in secrecy. (b) It was not a violation of duty or the rights of the public. (c) It was a form of revenue in which the government benefited. Because of this, the government was assisted in remunerating the officers. (d) It was not an embezzlement of government funds or public extortion. The author, however, notes that there have been some decadent periods in Vietnamese history when the mandarins took advantage of their right to expect presents. However, during the reigns of good monarchs they competed to do good according to Confucian standards, and even made their families proud because of their poverty.[56]

The interesting point made here is the distinction between the abuse and the proper practice of the traditional institution of remuneration by gifts. Once this distinction is made, it is not difficult to imagine how corruption crept in. However, we must examine the significance of the institution of the gift as a source of abuse in the causal network of corruption in view of the fact that many other socially approved practices have been infiltrated by corruption. In a society dominated by a corrupt regime any traditional institution capable of being abused is invaded by corruption, particularly by extortion. In traditional Malay society, to cite an instance, certain areas of abuse were conspicuous. These were the obligatory service for public welfare (*kerah*), gambling, entertainment and attempted acquaintance with ruling power. The abuse of the gift institution, placed in its proper context, is then to be seen as part of an ever widening circle of corruption. There is no reason to single this out as a particularly striking example of corruption. At the point where the abuse of this institution becomes an intolerable burden, it is seen to be part of a general epidemic of corruption. Corruption spreads and develops as a multiform phenomenon and it is impossible for us to assess one form or one source in isolation.

The exaggerated significance given to the gift institution and the role of traditional family ties should be re-examined in the light of contextual and historical analysis. If they were so dominant, it is baffling how certain Western countries have succeeded in restraining corruption despite the fact that socially approved traditional practices, theoretically vulnerable to an invasion by corruption, are still upheld. A valid explanation could be the breakdown of the feudal order and the rise of an impersonal and rational conception of the social order, supported by certain types of social change and social classes. But here this explanation breaks down. Within the context of the modern social order, and the familiar set of sociological factors invoked to explain the phenomenon as noted earlier, there has been the same process of expansion and contraction of corruption found in pre-modern society. The history of corruption in the United States is a convincing proof that corruption is not correlative with either pre-modern or modern conceptions of the bureaucracy, family ties, civic consciousness, the gift institution, or governmental ethics.

Furthermore, it is not true to presume that the demarcation line between corruption and proper conduct in underdeveloped societies is hazily drawn. If we take the Buddhist, Hindu or Islamic societies, we shall discover that there is a strong awareness and condemnation of corruption derived from the distinction between public and individual rights, and between right and wrong. Here I will give some examples from Islamic history, with which I am more familiar. Let me first cite the Quran, on the subject of bribing judges. 'And do not eat up your property among yourselves for vanities, nor use it as bait for the judges, with intent that ye may eat up wrongfully and knowingly a little of (other) people's property.'[57] The Quran insists that trustworthy people should be put in command, and that hatred or dislike for a party must not impede the execution of justice.[58]

Imam Ahmad ibn Hanbal (AD 780–855), the founder of one of the great schools of thought in Islam, was well known for his uncompromising attitude towards corruption and the abuse of power. He was beaten and imprisoned by the Caliph Mutasim for refusing to agree on some theological points. He abhorred the post of judge, and resented receiving presents from the palace so much that he severed communication with his sons for two or three months because they secretly accepted gifts and money from the Caliph. During his lifetime and even after his death he exerted a great influence on the Muslim world, and was revered by both Christians and Muslims during his lifetime.[59]

The clearest expression of an attitude against corruption was perhaps the boycott against the office of the *qadi* (judge). Many Muslim savants avoided accepting appointments as *qadi*. 'We are told how pious people hurried away from Mesopotamia across Syria to Arabia to escape their threatened appointments as judges; such, among others, were Sufyan Thauri, who died in concealment, and Abu Hanifa who, in spite of the lash, would not accept a judgeship. According to Tabari, the traditions taught by Abu Yusuf were suspect, because he was a friend of a *qadi*. Under Al-Mahdi the Qadi of Medina was made to accept the post by public flogging.'[60]

Almost every aspect of a *qadi*'s post was debated by pious scholars. Some maintained that the appointment should be paid, some that it should not. Our modern ideas on corruption, the separation between public and private property, efficiency, civic consciousness, scrupulousness and responsibility, were continuously present all through Islamic history, though they were not always successful in preventing corruption and decadence. An Egyptian judge appointed in AD 761 would himself make a deduction in his pay whenever he had to take time off to wash his clothes, attend a funeral, or do some other private work. To prevent corruption the Caliph Al-Hakim doubled the pay of a judge provided he did not receive a single *dirham* from the public.

The Maliki chief judge of Baghdad appointed in AD 915 accepted his appointment on the following conditions: (a) That he would not be approached on behalf of anyone; (b) that he would not be compelled to pass an illegal order; (c) that he would not accept a salary. Those who refused to accept a salary did so on principle. In AD 945, robbers broke into the house of the *Qadi* of Baghdad. Having found nothing in the house, they wanted to torture him. The *Qadi* fled to the roof and threw himself down to his death. Another Baghdad *qadi*, Abu Tayyib shared a turban and a coat with his brother—when one went out the other stayed at home. To these pious judges, their service was a sacred duty to the community and to God.

Even during this period, the onslaught of corruption was noticeable among the judges. In AD 961, the local ruler of Baghdad sold the office of chief justice for 200,000 *dirham* a year. The first purchaser was alleged to have combined an ugly figure with an ugly conduct. He was accused of pederasty, licentiousness and drink. But his success did not last. The Caliph refused to see him, and two years later he was removed from office. His successor nullified all his judgments on the grounds that he had bought his office.[61] Historically speaking it is apparent that there has always been a conflict between corruption and virtue, right up until the present day, especially in underdeveloped areas. An example from recent history is the effort of the African Muslim reformer and political leader Shehu Uthman Fodio, who was concerned with the Habe kingdoms in the eighteenth century. He attacked corrupt practices and the habit of giving presents.[62]

There are many instances of resistance against corruption from within a traditional framework, as well as examples of corrupt practices. It is not so much the institutional values that invite corruption, as other sociological factors. Hence it is doubtful whether we should focus the main explanatory observation on the traditional institution of the gift. What is often forgotten is also the fact that when the traditional societies of Asia and Africa came into contact with Western imperialism, many of them were already affected by corruption.[63] The influence of modernization does not come in at all. In some instances, the situation was aggravated by Western imperialism, but the corruption that followed has always been continuous with the past. Modernization and the rapid social changes accompanying it, when they invite corruption, do so in an already corrupt context. No doubt new problems are created and new forms of corruption emerge, but they do not justify an emphasis on these factors to the neglect of historical factors which may be more significant in an explanation.

THE PREVENTION OF CORRUPTION

The most important factor in the dynamics of corruption is the moral and intellectual stature of the leaders of the society. This suggestion should not be understood in a naïve sense. The moral and intellectual stature of the leaders becomes decisive and crucial within the configuration of other conditions. This factor has been noted by other students of corruption. What we are concerned with here is defining the pattern of relationships between the various conditioning factors of corruption, and to locate the position and function of leadership within that pattern.

We may note the following conditions which mitigate corruption, even if they do not effect an abolition: (a) A positive attachment to the government and a spiritual involvement in the task of national progress from both the public and the bureaucracy.[64] (b) Efficient administration and the proper structural adjustment of government machinery and regulation so as to avoid the creation of sources for corruption. (c) Favourable historical and sociological conditions. (d) The functioning of an anti-corruption value system. (e) The inspiring leadership of a group with high moral and intellectual standards. (f) An educated public with sufficient intelligence to appraise and follow the course of events.

The above conditions could be increased if we care to expand the historical and sociological conditions. We shall do so in the following case as an example, so as to be in the best position to see the pattern of relationships in the causal nexus of corruption.

In the history of British democracy, which was at one point seriously plagued by corruption, at least two mitigating factors were noticeable. During the eighteenth and nineteenth centuries, such factors were the rivalry between classes and the spiral inflation of corruption itself. Not only were votes paid for, but constituencies had been known to be sold to the highest bidder.[65] It, however, gradually became too expensive to buy the electorate.[66] The other factor was the invasion of the British Parliament by the *nabob*, also through corrupt means. If corruption had continued, it would eventually have led to the displacement of the ruling class in England by what Lord Chatham declared as 'people without connections, without any natural interest in the soil, the importers of foreign gold', who forced their way into Parliament through a torrent of corruption against which no private hereditary fortune could compete. Another set of sociological conditions, this time favourable to the growth of corruption, is the result of rapid structural changes in the social order like those associated with the industrialization process, particularly when these are preceded by decades of indifference to illegal practices and immorality.

The American scene in the late nineteenth century, and in subsequent decades, bears a strong causal resemblance to the underdeveloped countries. 'In the latter part of the nineteenth century, colossal fortunes were falling into the hands of the fortunate, and those who could not wait for them to fall were reaching up and grabbing them. Old laws failed to serve new purposes, and most legislators lacked the intelligence, even if they possessed the will, to regulate the dizzy processes of industrial expansion. Even the financier who wished to be law-abiding realized that legal paths were too indirect to serve his purpose, and it was easier to dole out bribes to politicians who were far from loath to share in the orgy of acquisition. The control of mineral lands, of water power, or of municipal franchises might mean the accumulation of gigantic fortunes in a short time, and it was no wonder that sharp-eyed businessmen, eager for wealth and power, ingeniously evaded or flauntingly defied the inadequate and feebly enforced laws of the land.'[67]

As regards the influence of government on the spread of corruption, the following factors are clearly contributive: (a) When government lets huge contracts containing terms which can bring fortunes to contractors. (b) When it collects very large sums of taxes hence offering temptations for bribes in exchange for tax reduction. (c) When it fixes rates for certain industries such as railroads, electricity and gas, as well as prices for a wide range of commodities. This leads to the dominant firms trying to control the rates and prices.

(d) When it exercises power to select who shall or shall not enter into an industry, as in the case of radio, television, interstate trucking, and aviation in the United States. (e) When it grants loans or permits for plants or equipment to be redeemed out of taxes over a short period of time. (f) When government subsidies are paid either openly or covertly.[68]

The above then are the potentially corruption-fraught areas of government activity. All the factors we have so far discussed are not in themselves operative unless there is a sufficient number of individuals who seize an opportunity for corruption. Within the configuration of these factors, the moral calibre of the individuals concerned is decisive. Similarly, no structural or legal changes in government administration designed to fight corruption will succeed, unless there is a sufficient number of individuals of high principle occupying key positions vital to the success of the effort.[69] The problem for a society desiring to get rid of corruption is precisely how to ensure a sufficient supply of such men and how to facilitate their rise to the vital positions.

During the era of the 'muckrakers' in America, the pioneers against corruption were men infused with a certain amount of idealism, courage, an intense hatred for injustice, a critical attitude towards the existing order, an optimism for success and confidence of the power of reason and justice. The role of these men in changing the morality of the period must not be underestimated. In Britain, for instance, there was never a period in the whole history of corruption in that country when there were not powerful forces fighting against it. The change in the historical and sociological context which discourages corruption can be translated into a living force only if there are effective and influential individuals to act as the catalysing agents. In the absence of such a group, corruption will obviously continue to thrive. How to ensure a society's steady supply of these individuals and to facilitate their rise to vital positions is always a central problem. Unfortunately sociology has hardly devoted any attention to this problem. Sociological and political studies of leadership, though fruitful in other aspects, have not significantly explored the area of corruption within ruling groups.

The point I wish to stress here is that since some attention has

35

been devoted to the general causes and conditions of corruption as well as its effects and since a great deal of existing findings can be accepted as valid, through explanation from historical, political, economic, sociological and anthropological analyses of corruption, we need not remain within the hitherto existing radius of explanation. We can extend our radius to include what has been neglected up to now. This is the influence of charismatic and sacral personalities in the daily life of the masses. In Asia, for instance, we can still rely on functioning traditional institutions for the creation of such personalities.

These saintly and charismatic religious personalities have been the most important single factor mitigating corruption throughout Asian history, during periods when no other resistance was available. They did not strive for power or wealth, and hence their positions amongst the masses were strengthened by their disinterestedness. Whether it is in Islam, Hinduism or Buddhism, these people were those who kept alive the tradition of organizing thought and action in terms of impersonal, universal, and achievement-oriented values. It is not true to say that all Asian tradition is ascription-oriented. There is a mixture of both orientations, but in terms of bureaucracy the Asian societies developed more on achievement-oriented values.

It is true that the goals of achievement have not always been identical with those of the modern West, but these goals have not been strictly essential for modernization. The essential goals for modernization, such as efficiency, rationality, sustained effort and hard work, constitute the Asian value system just as much as filial piety, religious devotion, kinship solidarity, etc. The difference between Asia and the West in historical development were caused by factors more significant than the value systems of their bureaucracies. One of the most traditional and feudal bureaucracies, namely, Japan, subsequently became a significant agent of modernization. If this feudalism and bureaucracy were completely devoid of achievement goals it would hardly be possible for Japan to transform itself into a modern, efficient oriented, industrialized society. It is a known fact that the modernization of Japan was initiated from above. The bureaucracy and the feudal lords played an active part in it after the earlier conflict with the feudal opposition section was resolved. The deification of the

Emperor Meiji illustrates the point we wish to stress, as the Emperor became the nation's paragon to which the people attributed everything good. The reverence shown to the Emperor was as to a deity.

In a different social setting in which factors found in the Japanese configuration are not present, as, for instance, in many underdeveloped countries, the sacral personalities have yet a role to perform. Though they have not the power to influence from above, as had the Japanese Emperor until the mid-twentieth century, they have nevertheless the influence to prevent moral anarchy and corruption. The influence of revered leaders on development has always inclined to the positive. To clarify their function further, let us relate it to the discussion of whether the system or the individual is the more significant cause in the development of corruption. We shall consider the views of two parties, Sorokin and Lunden, and Rogow and Lasswell.[70]

Sorokin and Lunden, in their study of power and morality, offer the following generalizations: (a) When the morality and mentality of rulers and the ruled are measured by the same moral and mental yardstick, then the ruler's morality and mind appear to be marked by a much stronger dualism, by greater mental and moral schizophrenia than the morality and mentality of the members of the ruled populations. (b) The ruling groups contain a large proportion of the extreme mental types of the gifted and the mentally sick than the rank and file of the ruled populations. (c) The moral behaviour of ruling groups tends to be more criminal and sub-moral than that of the ruled strata of the same society. (d) The greater, more absolute, and coercive the power of rulers, political leaders, and powerful business executives, labour and other organizations, and the less freely this power is approved by the ruled population, the more corrupt and criminal such ruling groups and executives tend to be. (e) With a progressive limitation of their power, criminality of rulers and executives tends to decrease.[71]

Sorokin and Lunden furnish us with some statistical data and discuss various aspects of the problem. The last two generalizations are of interest to us. It is suggested that the criminality of the rulers decreases in gravity and frequency with the limitation of their power. Thus democratic governments have a notably lower criminality than autocratic ones. If we take the crime of murder, particularly of relatives, for instance, the rate has been high. Of forty-three monarchs and Lord Protectors beginning with William I in England, and ending with George VI, about twenty rulers, or at least 40 per cent, were guilty of murder. With legal and factual limitation of the power of English monarchs their criminality accordingly decreased.

The data from the United States likewise points to a higher criminality among men in power. In 1923, ten leading American industrialists and financiers held a meeting in Edgewater Hotel in Chicago. Twenty-five years later in 1948, all of them had ended their careers tragically. At least four were convicted in court or had committed suicide. Sorokin and Lunden are inclined to agree with the Actonian generalization that power corrupts and absolute power corrupts absolutely.

It is Rogow and Lasswell who somehow challenged the truth of the above generalization. To my mind, their view is not a denial of Sorokin and Lunden's generalization. They only insist that power does not necessarily corrupt while Sorokin and Lunden stress the influence of the system on the spread and gravity of corruption and crime. Rogow and Lasswell have been successful but it does not invalidate Sorokin and Lunden's conclusion that the system is decisive in the frequency and gravity of the different types of crime.

Sorokin and Lunden published their work in 1959, while Rogow and Lasswell published theirs in 1963. The absence of reference to the former by the latter was probably due to the fact that both works were prepared at almost the same time. Now, after a lapse of more than three decades, we are in the position to furnish further data that increases the complexity of the problem. Accepting the validity of both approaches, we are still beset by the problem of causes. We have numerous instances in underdeveloped countries where the increase of crime and corruption has taken place within systems which theoretically should prevent such crimes. It is apparent that no matter how fool-proof such a system may be, unless the individuals in it are infused by the rectitude value, those systems may be abused and corrupted. We may here subscribe to the following generalization of Rogow and Lasswell: (a) If the leadership of the institution does not serve as a rectitude model, those belonging to, or serving in the institution may 'yield willingly or without much resistance'. (b) If the membership of an institution does not collectively enforce rectitude standards, the tendency towards individual corruption is increased. (c) Institutions of high and increasing prestige are more likely to attract ambitious men concerned with furthering their careers than corrupt men interested in promoting their personal fortunes. (d) Institutions declining in power or prestige are more likely to attract corrupt men interested in promoting their personal fortunes than ambitious men concerned with furthering their careers.[72]

It is apparent that the validity of Sorokin and Lunden's finding is relative to a certain context, and so is that of Rogow and Lasswell, who themselves emphasized the contextual approach. Now it is at this juncture, when a relatively adequate system is infested with corrupt power-holders, that the role of the charismatic sacral personalities should come into play. When the courts are dominated by corrupt judges, when the police become predatory, when Members of Parliament are corrupt and indifferent, when the leading influential figures abuse their power, when there is no group for the public to have recourse to, then the sacral personalities, who are devoid of power and wealth, can act as the centre of radiation of such rectitude values. They become the only influential embodiment of ideal rectitude. It matters not whether they are dead, and their emotional appeal is deeply rooted. Their teachings and precepts are transmitted in language intelligible to the multitude. Stories about their lives and teachings inspire towards rectitude.

The governments of underdeveloped countries should make greater effort to spread the influence of these personalities through schools and other institutions. They should also disseminate information of past efforts against corruption as developed within their traditional culture. Attempts of this sort should be considered as additional reinforcements to other means adopted in the fight against corruption, given that the goal is to achieve a just and equitable society. Because of the fact that such holy personalities can speak directly to the masses in familiar terms, their effectiveness is much greater than a dry philosophical discourse on justice. No great moral achievement in history has ever been accomplished by men whose source of inspiration is only what is provided by formal education. Great changes in history have been accomplished by men who have been inspired by other men. Whether it is the French Revolution, the American Revolution, the Russian Revolution, or the rise of the great religious civilizations, the inspiring influence of charismatic individual personalities transcending their times and places have all been the single decisive factor within a historical context.

Observers who do not participate in the actual day to day affairs of national development fail to realize the significance of individuals inspired by rectitude motives. It makes a great deal of difference to the country if a few courageous, efficient and honest individuals are occupying positions of power. This is particularly so when a country is in a precarious situation bordering on outright corruption, and, when a strong, articulate and aggressive public opinion against corruption has not yet crystallized. To form this public opinion the mediation of the sacral personalities is extremely functional.

There is another aspect to this problem in which the sacral personalities can contribute to attaching a stigma on to corruption. I suspect that one of the effective influences against corruption in Western European countries is the apprehension involved in accepting gifts entailing an obligation to return the favour. As Mauss points out, the gift not repaid debases a man who accepts it, especially if he does so with no intention of returning it. Mauss noted that in ancient Germanic languages the word 'gift' was used to denote both gift and poison. 'The theme of fateful gift, the present or possession that turns into poison, is fundamental in Germanic folklore. The Rhine Gold is fatal to the man who wins it, the Cup of Hagen is disastrous to the hero who drinks it; numerous tales and legends of this kind, Germanic and Celtic, still haunt our imagination.'[73]

The danger of accepting gifts was also felt in Oriental culture. We have already noted Imam Ahmad Ibn Hanbal's abhorrence of receiving gifts. An anxiety involved in the acceptance of gifts has been observed in many countries all over the world. It does not seem to be a difficult step to extend this sense of apprehension to affect the accepting of a bribe. We may thus claim that the traditional institution of the gift can

40

work against bribery. The weakening of this element against corruption in Asian history was often caused by the ruling groups. The sages and the sacral personalities were powerless, but they derived merit from the fact that they kept alive the ideal against corruption. There has always been a continuous denunciation of corruption throughout Asian history.

A Digambara Jain teacher of the tenth century denounced bribery as the door through which all manner of sin would enter. In the teachings of Buddhism, bribery is equally condemned as stealing, cheating and killing. Sikhism, Hinduism and Islam all say the same thing. The rectitude trend failed to dominate because the rulers were not interested in it. The authors of the *Huai-nan Tzu*, a philosophical work of the early Han period said to be compiled at the court of Liu Ann, grandson of the first Han emperor, around 122 BC aptly described the decisive influence of rulers in the promotion of rectitude values, or vices. 'The power to achieve success or failure,' it says, 'lies with the ruler. If the measuring-line is true, then the wood will be straight, not because one makes a special effort, but because that which it is "ruled" by makes it so. In the same way if the ruler is sincere and upright, then honest officials will serve in his government and scoundrels will go into hiding, but if the ruler is not upright then evil men will have their way and loyal men will retire to seclusion. Why is it that people often scratch melons or gourds with their fingernails, but never scratch stones or jewels? Because no matter how hard they scratch stones or jewels they can never make an impression. In the same way if the ruler can be made to adhere to right, maintain fairness, and follow a measuring-line, as it were, in measuring high and low, then even though his ministers come to him with evil designs it will be the same as dashing eggs against a rock or throwing fire into water. King Ling loved slim waists and all the women went on diet and starved themselves. The King of Yueh admired bravery and all the men outdid each other in dangerous feats defying death. From this we may see that he who wields authority can change the customs and transform the manner of his people.'[74]

It was sacral personalities like Mahavira, Buddha, Christ, Muhammad, Nanak, Kabir, Ramakrishna, and numerous others, who inspired the scholars and sages to unceasingly maintain ideals of rectitude. It would be a great mistake to ignore their contribution and their relevance to contemporary problems of restraining corruption in underdeveloped countries. Those aspects of their teachings touching upon corruption should be emphasized, if the governments of the underdeveloped countries are really concerned with the problem of eliminating corruption and employing all means at their disposal against it. In the light of a contextual and historical analysis, it appears that the Asian traditions contain values and articulate trends against bureaucratic corruption as well as other forms of corruption. It also reveals a certain degree of awareness as to the causes and function of corruption.

Endnotes

1. *Sinar Harapan*, Djakarta, 28 August 1967. The issue of 3 September 1967, suggested the involvement of three parties in this affair, the bank officials, the army officer and the suppliers. A photocopy of the cheque.

2. *Ibid.*, 16 September 1967.

3. *Ibid.*, 28 August 1967.

4. *Ibid.*, 11 August 1967.

5. *Ibid.*, 6 September 1967.

6. *Ibid.*, 7 September 1967.

7. J. S. Nye, 'Corruption and Political Development: A Cost Benefit Analaysis', *The American Political Science Review*, June 1967, vol. LXI, no. 2.

8. Wang An Shih, 'Memorial of a Myriad Words' (Wan Yen Shu), in H. R. Williamson, *Wang An Shih*, A. Probsthain, London, 1935, vol. 2, p. 75.

9. See Ibn Khaldun, *The Muqaddimah*, 3 vols., tr. F. Rosenthal, Routledge and Kegan Paul, London, 1958 (vol. 2 is of special interest).

10. An instance at hand is B. Noggle's *The Teapot Dome*, Louisiana State University Press, Baton Rouge 1962. This is primarily a historical work. As a source of sociology insight, it is interesting although it does not furnish an analysis of the subject.

11. A. A. Rogow and H. D. Lasswell, *Power, Corruption, and Rectitude*, Prentice Hall, New Jersey, 1963. This is a stimulating work against the Actonian generalization that power corrupts. It also deals with other aspects of power and corruption of interest to the sociology of corruption.

12. W. F. Wertheim, 'Sociological Aspects of Corruption in Southeast Asia', in his *East–West Parallels*, Van Hoeve, The Hague, 1965.

13. W. F. Wertheim, *op. cit.*, p. 105.

14. The term 'criminal', as used in this book, is not meant to be taken in the sense of a subjective value judgement. The criteria of evaluation are those upheld by the societies referred to, in our present context, Asia and the West. Their roots are to be found in the great religions such as Islam, Christianity, Buddhism and Hinduism, and in all the humanistic traditions of the Western world. There is a wide range of agreement on fundamental values, and it is these values that serve as criteria to distinguish criminal behaviour from non-criminal behaviour.

15. One avenue for fraud is the claiming of excessive mileage allowance. This is usually done by increasing the frequency of trips, in the performance of duty. A civil service system like that of Malaysia or Singapore which allows mileage claims will have to face the problem of fraud in this respect.

16. Though we are here concerned with corruption involving government officials or officials of other public institutions, our concept of corrupt behaviour should not accordingly be restricted to such an instance. We can have corruption between public and public, as in the case of the bribery of voters by election candidates. But this is also a form of deception where the law of the country prohibits such practice.

17. 'A corrupt act violates responsibility towards at least one system of public or civic order and is, in fact, incompatible with (destructive of) any such system. A system of public or civic order exalts common interest over special interest; violations of the common interest for special advantage are corrupt.' A. A. Rogow and H.D. Lasswell, *op. cit.*, p. 132.

18. For instance, see Myron Weiner, *The Politics of Scarcity*, University of Chicago Press, Chicago, 1962; Herbert J. Spiro, *Politics in Africa*, Prentice Hall, New Jersey, 1962; O. P. Dwivedi, 'Bureaucratic Corruption in Developing Countries', *Asian Survey*, April 1967, vol.VII, no. 4, N. H. Leff, 'Economic Development through Bureaucratic Corruption', *The American Behavioral Scientist*, November 1964, vol. VII, no. 3; Colin Leys, 'What is the Problem about Corruption?', *The Journal of Modern African Studies*, 1965, vol.III, no. 2, and D. H. Bailey, 'The Effects of Corruption in a Developing Nation', *The Western Political Quarterly*, December 1966, vol. 19.

19. 'And while traditional gift-giving can be distinguished from a bribe of money, it is quite obvious that from the point of view of the giver the one has shaded into the other, so that although the practice has taken on a new significance, as the open gift of a chicken is replaced by a more furtive gift of a pound note, it is nevertheless an established fact of life, in which the precise nature of the rule-infringement is partially concealed by continuity with an older custom.' C. Leys, *op. cit.*, p. 225.

20. W. F. Wertheim, *op. cit.*, p. 125.

21. Myron Weiner, *op. cit.*, p. 121.

22. *Ibid.*, p. 235. Weiner recognized the detrimental effect of corruption but saw it as not altogether detrimental.

23. This gentleman is sufficiently well-versed in Islamic thought and history. It is possible that he is aware of Muslim thought on corruption. Mustafa Ibn Abdullah, known as Katib Chelebi (AD 1609–57), the Turkish scholar, had written an article on bribery and referred to earlier sources. Bribery was classified into (a) that which was forbidden for both parties, and (b) that which was forbidden to one party, namely the receiver. The latter was approved if the intention was to avoid harm. See Katib Chelebi, *The Balance of Truth*, tr. G. Lewis, Allen and Unwin, London, 1957.

24. C. Leys, *op. cit.*, p. 222. His source is the Uganda Parliamentary Debates, 8, 11, November 1963. Corruption was alleged by the opposition. Leys's article is quite interesting and provoking though vulnerable to certain criticisms.

25. Leys is definitely aware of this, as expressed in his article.

26. Leys, *op.cit.*, pp. 220–1.

27. See *Ibid.*, pp. 221–4. There is some ambiguity in his use of the concept. Apparently he also employs a non-relativistic stand which is undefined when he states 'Corruption is relatively easy to conceal in the new states'. What is the kind of corruption he has in mind here? That which is defined by the actor or the observer?

28. J. J. Senturia, 'Political Corruption', in *Encyclopaedia of the Social Sciences*, vols. 3–4, 1960.

29. The above data on Latin America are derived from an excellent and stimulating study: Stanislav Andreski, *Parasitism and Subversion*, Weidenfeld and Nicolson, London, 1966.

30. *Ibid.*, p. 67.

31. *Ibid.*, pp. 67–8.

32. The father of a student in the country's leading university informed me that it became an accepted practice for the students to contribute rice to the teachers. In addition to this the students offered piles of old newspapers which the teachers would sell. The teachers were frequently absent from class.

33. From the point of view of typology, this is an interesting novelty. This form of extortive corruption is indirect, collective and unconscious. There is no conscious transaction between individuals, giver and receiver. The victims cannot be said to be involved in corruption. This instance has not been widely confirmed.

34. According to the former Chief Minister of Sabah (East Malaysia), some timber tycoons were interested in his removal from office at the time when he was heading the state administration because they did not like his policy of renewing timber licences. He alleged that the annual licence lobby had strong political influence. *The Straits Times*, 16 June 1967.

35. N. H. Leff, *op.cit.*, p. 11.

36. The Malaysian Minister of Commerce and Industry, Dr Lim Swee Aun had warned the pioneer industries that their tariff protection would be taken away if they abused it. He cited the cement industry as an example. Following an outcry of overproduction by the manufacturers, the government raised the import duty of foreign cement from RM12 to RM24 per ton in 1966, to give the local industry protection. However, the local industry raised the price of cement from RM52 to RM72 per ton. The Minister reacted by reverting to the previous import duty of RM12 per ton. Thereby withdrawing the protection, after unsuccessfully attempting to get the local industry to reduce the price. He stated in Parliament that the government would take action against any industry which attempted to exploit the consumer by taking advantage of the protection (*The Straits Times*, 22 June 1967). In a country totally gripped by corruption there would not be such a minister implementing an anti-exploitation policy. The exploitation would continue.

37. *Malaysian Official Yearbook*, 1964, Government Printing Press, Kuala Lumpur, 1966, vol. 4, p. 336.

38. The Malaysian Parliament has recognized the presence of corruption and the need to tighten the anti-graft law so as to widen the scope of people and activity liable to be punished for corruption. In the last session of Parliament certain allegations of corruption were made against some co-operative societies of government officers and one such society of the university staff. *The Straits Times*, 22 June 1967.

39. Factory X in Malaysia has been producing for years article Y of vital public necessity. The imported article Y costs about twice that manufactured by factory X. The quality, however, is at least twice better than the locally manufactured one. For the past several years no improvement of the local article has been noticed. If the import duty on the imported article were reduced so that the price is more or less equal to that of factory X, a genuine competitive setting would then be created, and in this setting factory X, a genuine competitive setting would then be created, and in this setting factory X would disappear from the market. No amount of corruption will make people prefer its product. In an under-developed area the setting has always been (a) protection of local industry, or (b) competition between unequal contenders, foreign and local. Whichever is the setting, corruption has never contributed positively to their efficiency.

40. N. H. Leff, *op.cit.*, p. 11.

41. Neither the details nor the source were given of this instance. Other instances were referred to an expert in Latin American economic development, probably through personal contact. See N. H. Leff, *op.cit.*, pp. 11–12, and note 7, p. 14.

42. S. Andreski, *op.cit.*, pp. 230–1.

43. *Ibid.*, p. 231. The details on Peron's economic policy, in preceding paragraphs, are also derived from here.

44. *Ibid.*

45. See O. P. Dwivedi, *op. cit.*, pp. 251–3. The author suggests some positive influences of corruption, one of which is what he calls universalistic bribery advocated to replace ascriptive corruption.

46. S. Andreski, *op. cit.*, p. 69. 'It must be remembered, however, that just as a body can tolerate a certain number of bacteria without suffering much harm, but succumbs to them once the white corpuscles can no longer keep them in check, so a society which can withstand sporadic graft suffers severe deformations once it becomes brazen and widespread.'

47. For a further detailed discussion, see Ralph Braibanti, 'Reflections on Bureaucratic Corruption', *Public Administration*, vol. 40, no. 4, 1962.

48. *Ibid.*, p. 358.

49. *Ibid.*

50. See an earlier reference in this paper to the views of Leys and Wertheim. For Sprio's view see his book, *op. cit.*, p. 103.

51. O. P. Dwivedi, *op. cit.*, p. 248. He was referring to the Indian example, how the norm of solidarity of the extended family is transferred to the civil service.

52. J. van den Brand, *De Millioenen uit Delhi*, Pretoria, Amsterdam, 1902. Quoted by Wertheim, *op. cit.*, p. 118. According to Wertheim and Furnivall, corruption in the Netherlands Indies was, following this period, at its lowest. It was practically unknown, much in contrast with Burma. See J. S. Furnivall, *Colonial Policy and Practice*, New York University Press, New York, 1956, p. 269.

53. This practice in on the increase in Malaysia.

54. Chitoshi Yanaga, *Japanese People and Politics*, John Wiley, New York, 1956, pp. 317–18.

55. Nghiem Dang, *Vietnam, Politics and Public Administration*, East–West Center Press, Honolulu, 1966, p. 268.

56. *Ibid.*

57. Abdullah Yusuf Ali (tr. ed.), *The Holy Quran*, Ashraf, Lahore, 1938, vol. 1, 2:188, pp. 74–5.

58. *Ibid.*, 4:58, pp. 197–8, and 5:9, p. 243.

59. W. M. Patton, *Ahmed ibn Hanbal and the Minha*, Brill, Leiden, 1897, pp. 178–9. 'He had a profound dislike to the receiving of money assistance from others, and took very little pains to secure money for himself. His happiest moments were those when he was left without a coin in his purse.'

60. A. Mez, *The Renaissance of Islam*, tr. S. Khuda Baksh, D. D. Margoliouth, Jubilee Publishing House, Patna, 1937. p. 219.

61. *Ibid.*, p. 223.

62. On his theory of government see M. Hiskett, 'Kitab Al-Farq: A Work on the Habe Kingdoms Attributed to Uthman and Fodio', *Bulletin of the School of Oriental and African Studies*, University of London, 1960, vol. 23, pp. 558–79.

63. Chinese scholars and historians had been aware of this problem. In numerous instances their views were interesting and instructive. Wang Fu-chih (1619–92), a philosopher of depth and power, noted the ever recurring corruption of the ruling dynasties and governments so much so that even the wisest sovereign would find it difficult to effect a speedy reform. It is regrettable that the historical trend of many contemporary sociologists studying Asian problems, particularly corruption, has ignored the discussions of Asian scholars on the subject. For the Chinese views, see W. T. de Bary, Wing-tsit Chan and B. Watson (eds.), *Sources of Chinese Traditions*, Columbia University Press, New York, 1961.

64. W. F. Wertheim, *op. cit.*, p. 130.

65. Ronald Wraith and Edgar Simpkins, *Corruption in Developing Countries*, Allen and Unwin, London, 1963, p. 66.

66. For more details on this, see W. B. Gwyn, *Democracy and the Costs of Politics in Britain*, Athlone Press, London, 1962.

67. C. C. Reiger, *The Era of the Muckrakers*, Peter Smith, Gloucester, Massachusetts, 1957, pp. 2–3.

68. P. H. Douglas, *Ethics in Government*, Harvard University Press, Cambridge, Massachusetts, 1952, pp. 22–3.

69. Chu Cheng-po, in his memorial submitted in 1895 after China's defeat by Japan, emphasized the basic weakness, the incompetence and venality of officials. He said, 'In the present world our trouble is not that we lack good institution, but that we lack upright minds. If we seek to reform institutions, we must first reform men's minds. Unless all men of ability assist each other, good laws, become mere paper documents; unless those who supervised them are fair and enlightened, the venal will end up occupying the places of the worthy.' W. T. de Bary, Wing-tsit Chan and B. Watson, *op. cit.*, p. 737.

70. The views of the two parties are complementary. They illustrate respectively the

different aspects of the problem. Taking their writings as a whole, they assimilated each other's position. The presentation here is not to be taken in the sense of two opposite theories but as two complementary treatments of the same problem.

71. P. A. Sorokin, and W. A. Lunden, *Power and Morality*, Porter Sargent, Boston, 1959, pp. 36–7.

72. A. A. Rogow and H. D. Lasswell, *op. cit.*, pp. 58–9. As apparent from earlier and following references, the views of Sorokin, Lunden, Lasswell and Rogow, have been anticipated by Asian thinkers centuries earlier. The interesting point is the increasing awareness of the complexity of the problem and the depth of analysis developed by modern social scientists.

73. Marcel Mauss, *The Gift*, tr. I. Cunnison, Cohen and West, London, 1954, p. 62.

74. W. T. de Bary, Wing-tsit Chan and B. Watson, *op. cit.*, pp. 177–8.

Chapter 2

CORRUPTION IN ASIA: THE HUMAN COST

CORRUPTION has inflicted suffering upon human society from time immemorial. From ancient Near East, Greece, Rome, China and India, we have ample evidence of the prevalence of corruption. Ancient China and the Roman Empire provide striking materials of it. Corruption affected their history in no small way. The frequent wars, the violent overthrows of ruling powers, the disorganization and breakdowns of societies, have always been related to corruption. It became crucial to the break-up of these societies in combination with other causes.

Corruption is essentially the abuse of trust in the interest of personal and private gain. When a public servant violates the norms of his duty in the interest of another party in return for inducement in monetary or other forms, he is said to have committed a corrupt act. It is an intentional violation of duty with the motive of gaining personal advantage by receiving a bribe or other benefits from a party in need of a particular decision affecting interests the public servant can bring about.

In the first chapter of this book, I divided corruption into three types—the extortive, the manipulative and the nepotistic. Nepotism refers to the appointment of relatives or friends to positions for which they are not qualified thereby injuring the interest of the institution and those who are qualified. We shall not be concerned with this type of corruption here. Our concerns are the extortive and manipulative types of corruption. Extortive corruption refers to a situation where one is forced to bribe, to defend, or gain one's rights or needs. Manipulative corruption refers to the attempt to influence decisions in one's favour, in any area of life.

If a social order is highly infected by corruption its level of welfare would then be very low. The reason for this is that corruption has such a devastating effect on the smooth running of a government administration. We are not concerned here with corruption as a clandestine, isolated, activity involving small groups of people outside the main centres of power. What we are concerned with is what I propose to call 'tidal corruption'. It is a corruption that floods the entire state apparatus involving those at the centre of power. Like the tide, it rises to cover wider areas and immerse the surrounding vegetation.

The extent and depth of corruption is visible to anyone interested in the subject. In a highly corrupt country practically all government public services involve corruption. There is a minority who by virtue of its position or influence is not subject to corruption. The rise in population further promotes corruption in the sense that it increases the demand for goods and services. The more the demand the more the corruption.

In the developing countries of Asia, the ruling groups manage to retain their power for nearly a generation if not longer. In most of these countries it takes more than twenty years to change a ruling group, if there is any change at all. Even if there is a change, the succeeding group is not of a different mentality as far as corruption is concerned. The stability of a corrupt regime thus helps to consolidate and intensify its corruption. This is a serious dilemma. It is true that Asia needs stable governments, but a government that becomes a tool of corruption would only convert that stability into an obstructive and destructive force inimical to development.

The period of Asian history I am concerned with is that after World War II. The war and the independence of Asian countries from Western rule figure prominently in the outburst of corruption characterizing the post-war period. Under colonial rule there was corruption but its dynamics and phenomenology took a drastic turn following the independence of the country. This drastic turn was mainly due to: (a) widespread corruption during the war period preceding the achievement of independence, (b) the sudden increase in administration, (c) the sudden increase in opportunities for corruption at a bigger and higher scale, (d) the invasion of the different levels of leadership by people of low moral integrity, (e) the inexperience of leaders fighting for independence in building a clean and efficient government, and (f) the manipulation and intrigues of foreign financial and business powers through means of corruption.

THE CASE OF INDIA

The case of India is instructive from the above point of view. In 1962, several Members of Parliament referred to the growing menace of corruption in the administration. A committee was formed by the then Minister of Home Affairs, Lal Bahadur Shastri, headed by a Member of Parliament, K. Santhanam. The final report of the committee, called the Santhanam Report, was handed to the government on 31 March 1964. What concerns us here is the analysis of the causes of corruption and the measures suggested to prevent it. We shall select those parts relevant to our purpose. Henceforth this document shall be referred to as 'the Report'.

First, there is the difference between the past and present bureaucracies: 'In primitive and medieval societies the scope of public authority was small; many of the matters that were looked after by the community have now become a function of the state. The few authorities which existed for the collection of taxes, administration of justice or other purposes did not act according to any definite written laws or rules, but largely at their discretion subject to good conscience and equity and directives from the higher authorities. So long as the officials were loyal to the existing regime and did not resort to oppression and forcible expropriation, they were free to do as they liked.'[1]

Next, the corruptive influence of World War II: 'The immense war efforts during 1939 to 1945 which involved an annual expenditure of hundreds of crores of rupees over all kinds of war supplies and contracts created unprecedented opportunities for acquisition of wealth by doubtful means. The wartime controls and scarcities provided ample opportunities for bribery, corruption, favouritism, etc. The then

51

government subordinated all other considerations to that of making the war effort a success. Propriety of means was no consideration if it impeded the war effort. It would not be far wrong to say that the high water mark of corruption was reached in India as perhaps in other countries also, during the period of the Second World War.'[2]

Before the war, according to the Report, corruption was prevalent among the low level officials. The higher ranks were comparatively free of it. Lack of fluid resources set limits to the opportunities and capacity for corruption. After the transfer of power at the time of independence, there was patriotism and high ideals. Attempts were made to check the spread of corruption. But it was thwarted by: 'Yet, various factors have operated to nullify in some measure the anti-corruption drive. The sudden extension of the economic activities of the government with a large armoury of regulations, controls licenses and permits provided new and large opportunities. The quest for political power at different levels made successful achievement of the objective more important than the means adopted. Complaints against the highly placed in public life were not dealt with in the manner that they should have been dealt with if public confidence had to be maintained. Weakness in this respect created cynicism and the growth of the belief that while governments were against corruption they were not against corruption individuals, if such individuals had the requisite amount of power, influence, and protection.'[3]

The rapid urbanization brought about the weakening of rural values. Social controls resulting in the maintenance of frugality and simplicity of life were replaced by those encouraging materialism, impersonalism, status craving, greed for money and power, and an unwillingness to adhere to moral values. In this climate, the business and commercial classes, whose ranks were swelled by speculators and adventurers of the war period, exerted their corruptive influence. The salaried classes meanwhile experienced a decline in real income. A large part of these classes belonged to government service. All these formed a fertile soil for corruption.

There was also the cumbersome and dilatory procedures and practices in the working of government offices. This gave rise to the 'speed money' type of corruption. 'Generally the bribe giver does not wish, in these cases, to get anything done unlawfully, but wants to speed up the process of the movement of files and communications relating to decisions. Certain sections of the staff concerned are reported to have got into the habit of not doing anything in the matter till they are suitably persuaded.'[4]

The scope and incentives for corruption were greatest at the points where important decisions that would substantially affect the fortunes of interested groups or individuals, were taken: such as in the assessment and collection of taxes, obtaining licences, contracts, or in orders of supplies. It was suggested that the corruption cost was between 7 and 11 per cent in undertakings done for the government.[5] The Report finally took into account businessmen and industrialists as the greatest corrupting influences on a major and organized scale. 'To these, corruption is not only an easy method to secure large unearned profits but also the necessary means to enable them to be in a position to pursue their vocations or retain their position among their own competitors. It is these persons who indulge in evasion and avoidance of taxes, accumulate large amounts of unaccounted money by various methods such as obtaining licences in the names of bogus firms and individuals, trafficking in licences, suppressing profits by manipulation of accounts to avoid taxes and other legitimate claims on profits, accepting money for transactions put through without accounting for it in bills and accounts (on-money) and under-valuation of transactions in immovable property. It is they who have control over large funds and are in a position to spend considerable sums of money in entertainment. It is they who maintain an army of liaison men and contact men, some of whom live, spend and entertain ostentatiously. We are unable to believe that so much money is being spent only for the purpose of getting things done quickly.'[6]

The Report further mentioned the activity of these contact men to subvert the integrity of government servants. 'The tendency to subvert integrity in the public services instead of being isolated and aberrative is growing into an organized, well-planned racket.'[7] In addition to such attempts there was the offer of employment to retired government servants by the commercial and industrial sector. 'It is generally believed that such employment is secured in many cases as a *quid pro quo* for favours shown by the government servant while in service. It is also feared that highly placed government servants may be in a position, by virtue of their past standing, to exercise undue influence on government servants in service who might have been their colleagues or subordinates. The fact that some of these retired government servants who have accepted employment with private firms live in Delhi and perhaps operate as "contact men" has further heightened these suspicions.'[8]

The Report was written amidst a surrounding of corruption which had even gone to the schools, colleges and the courts. It had reached such proportions that a large majority of people doubted whether it could be eradicated. Corruption was all pervasive. 'In our country,' said Dr S. Radhakrishnan, who was then President of India, 'moral life is shaken to its foundations. Love of wealth and power has gained wide acceptance. Most of us live on the surface of life with no moral earnestness.'[9] There is hardly any corner of Indian life which has not been defiled by corruption.

Let us start with the houses of worship. A colossal amount of gold and grain were donated to these houses of worship. Some, no doubt, was used for maintaining the shrines, providing relief for the poor, assistance for pilgrims and money for the salaries of temple workers. But a good deal was embezzled, systematically and cynically. The most dumbfounding incident was the disappearance of 40,000 acres of land belonging to the Brihadeswara temple in Thanjavur, Tamil Nadu.[10] Both Hindu and Muslim religious endowments were attacked by corruption.

All sections of government bureaucracy had been infected with corruption. Some high police officials auctioned remunerative police stations to the highest bidding subordinates. Some jailers broke prison rules. One government agency bribed and swindled another. Elections were full of fraud. Leading smugglers helped the political parties in elections. This rapid increase of corruption in India gave smuggling and other criminal gangs a foothold in Indian society. The illegally earned money they accumulated was converted into lawful use through legitimate business.

The smugglers had set up a huge and powerful undertaking. This undertaking paralleled government in its area of operations. The smugglers had at their disposal fleets of vessels, counter-intelligence networks, thousands of carriers, armed men, social security systems, insurance companies, and a banking system. Smuggling on such a gigantic scale could not have been carried out without the connivance of influential politicians and bureaucrats.[11]

Agents were encouraged to obtain government assistance to open poultry farms near landing creeks used for dumping contraband. One smuggler had a 44.72-hectare farm in front of a customs house where contraband goods were dumped.[12] In the words of an author, 'Smuggling in India is not a fringe economic activity of a few persons in search of easy affluence. It is an industry—a sub-economic system—in which the Congress and the rest of the power elite comprising lakhs of people—big and small—have a vital interest.'[13]

The black marketeers also had their influence in Indian politics. They joined a political party, became office bearers, and eventually controlled the party. They donated to the parties which did not have independent sources of income. Once entrenched, the black marketeers would seize any available opportunity; the disposal of goods illegally produced, theft of relief food or other materials, hoarding and the release of selected commodities, and trade in money. Black marketing operations were more significant apparently in iron, steel, cloth, cotton yarn, man-made fibres, cement, fertilizers, aluminium, sugar, molasses, motor vehicles, coal and paper. Scarcity of goods, coupled with dishonest industrial practices to perpetuate the scarcity, was the main cause of the black market operation which assumed staggering heights after the mid-1960s.[14]

THE COST OF CORRUPTION

The Indian black market with its smuggling operation is characteristic of the pattern of corruption with foreign exchange and import control. The inhumanity resulting from corruption in a country already facing serious problems in fulfilling the minimum requirements of daily living, is too horrible to imagine. Consider food relief in times of famine deflected to the black market at the cost of human lives. Consider the adulteration of vital drugs which leave patients of serious diseases untreated. Consider the corruption in schools, what it did to the minds of the students.

The students are introduced into the world of corruption at a young age. Principals usually prefer children of parents who can dispense patronage or favours, as well as those who can pay. A list of rich children in each class is maintained and they are sought after for the purpose of selling fund-raising tickets. 'In some schools teachers squeeze out gifts from students. The good old practice of giving flowers to the teacher has been replaced by giving her a watch, an imported pen, lipstick and even a sari.'[15]

The events described here are from Delhi, the capital of India. Those who register for school far outnumber the available vacancies. Nevertheless registration is not discouraged for it brings revenue due to the fees. Admissions are not based on the results of the written test. At times questions are leaked out to certain people the school wishes to oblige, or marks are raised. The illegal fees without receipt vary between Rs2,000 and Rs12,000, depending on the prestige of the school.

Children who fail the annual examinations are promoted after the vacation by the principal. Such are the perks for those who are in the corrupt assembly. For those who are not yet dragged into the assembly, low marks are deliberately given to force them to get outside tuition. Wives of government officials, journalists, or police officials, from whom the school may hope for return favours, find it easier to get jobs than a serious and brilliant BA graduate.

Admission to the university is also a big racket. Eighty per cent admission to the university is on merit and the other 20 per cent is reserved for the scheduled caste and outstanding sportsmen who have represented the state. However, this rule is abused to suit the corrupt. 'In every college in Delhi University, it is estimated that 20 per cent of the admissions are on bogus certificates. Boys from influential families and student leaders who have failed to make the merit list get a certificate stamped by a Councillor that he is a scheduled caste. This is registered at the Deputy Commissioner's office by paying a small bribe to the clerk on duty. Children of well known leaders got admission on these bogus certificates. When they were caught, the file containing the bogus certificates could not be traced.'[16]

The use of bogus credentials, the tampering with examination marks, the manipulation of admission requirements, are all fairly prevalent. The same state prevails in the courts. According to the estimate of an advocate, 95 per cent of the staff in the lower courts are corrupt. One mode of bribing a judge is to sell coveted goods at a low price. Thus, an imported television set originally bought for Rs7,000 on the black market is sold to the judge for Rs3,000.

In the transportation and building industries, corruption has one of the most fertile soils. Here the corrupt elements in the opposition parties also share the spoils. What is called 'hush money' is paid to the opposition not to expose violations of the construction laws. A whole network and organization is set up for the huge corruption syndicate. Bureaucratic positions favourable to corruption are referred to as 'wet posts'. An officer is supposed to stay not more than three years in such a post. However some stay much longer because they can function as stooges for councillors or bureaucrats.[17]

In a society totally gripped by corruption, everything that is possible to corrupt is seized for the purpose. The forms and manifestations of corruption are beyond description. New ideas are continually added. Corruption becomes an industry. Like an industry it seeks to create a public demand. Hence new rules and legislations are added to existing ones for the purpose of corruption. Every time a new rule or law is created and public dependence on officials is required, it is a welcome source of corruption.

A clear instance of this kind of manipulation is the size of the passport. Passports are made thinner and smaller so that more can be squeezed from the public who need them. In highly corrupt countries, it is not easy to get a passport. The sooner the passport is used up or expires, the better it is. This is, of course, not easy to prove for there are always other reasons offered.

The climate created by corruption favours the luxurious growth of an innumerable variety of crimes, including murder. Thus a student in Pakistan killed an invigilating teacher who detected him copying from notes illegally brought into the examination hall. In another case, a private tutor attempted to impersonate a student and appeared in the examinations. This tutor was apprehended and subsequently convicted.[18]

The relation between crime and corruption is well-documented. But more serious than the extortion racket organized by criminal syndicates is the extortion carried out by government servants. In a corrupt society, extortion is the order of the day. Extortive corruption is the most prevalent type of corruption. It is also the most pernicious type when innocent members of the public become its victims. Extortion spreads into the various professions once it is all pervasive in government administration.

The nature of this extortion is complex. The rich and fertile imagination of the wives of corrupt officials furnished yet innumerable patterns woven into the fabric of extortion. The husbands are already busy squeezing the main juice but the wives manage to squeeze further ingredients from the source. An interesting instance is a case of alphonzo mangoes from Bombay. A senior industrial executive in Rajasthan parcelled locally obtained mangoes in such a manner as to make it appear that the parcel was sent from Bombay and presented it to the wife of a secretary of a ministry because the said lady yearned for mangoes from Bombay.[19]

Another form of corruption executed through extortion is the use of official servants for private purposes, a situation highly cherished by wives of officials. An aged bureaucrat complained that some servants refused to wash dishes and undergarments of ladies. They must be made to co-operate through fear of termination of service or through temptation of extra money, food or accommodation. He said that the use of official servants at home enhances the prestige of the ladies in the eyes of other women.[20]

As stated earlier the forms and manifestations of corruption are so numerous that it would be impossible for us to discuss them in their totality. What we shall do here is to give some random illustrations as background to the discussion to follow on the effects of corruption. These illustrations have been selected from India, not because India is considered as the most corrupt, but only because the Indian materials are readily available. Furthermore, my impression is that the corruption problem has been most discussed and written about in books in India, more than in any other Asian country. The venality and rapacity of corruption in Pakistan, Bangladesh, Indonesia, the Philippines and Thailand, to mention some of the countries with a high degree of corruption, are as serious as those of India.

In terms of efforts to wipe out corruption, though far from successful, India appears to be more active than the other Asian countries mentioned. The *modus operandi* arising from the Indian experience are generally the same as in other Asian countries. So are the types of corruption. The boldness with which corruption is executed is also striking in some instances. There are differences concerning the targets of corruption, such as the government-owned oil company Pertamina in Indonesia, and the kind of political system intertwined with the corruption activity. As far as *modus operandi* are concerned, there is a great deal of similarity.

According to M. Halayya, of the three Indian defence services, the Army, the Navy and the Air Force, the Amy is the least corrupt. Corruption in the army is most pronounced in the supply section. The Army Supply Corps unit handles on an average five to seven million kilograms of various types of food articles, and of these fresh vegetables alone constitute about a million kilograms. 'Officers in charge of processing these supplies will not accept the fresh ration from the contractors unless the latter grease the palm of the former to an adequate extent, no matter how exactly the fresh ration conforms to the specimen ration. The contractors are kept in constant fear that the highly perishable fresh ration may be rejected in which case the loss will be thousands of rupees and, in certain cases, even lakhs.'[21]

THE CASE OF MALAYSIA

This reminds me of irregularities of supply for the Malaysian Army in East Malaysia. One concerned instant noodles, for the period of January 1977 to December 1978. The contract prices were RM4.90 and RM3.90 respectively per packet while the average price in Peninsular Malaysia for that period was only 14 sen. The Ministry of Defence had really been cheated. The government could have saved RM962,000 had this item been bought in the peninsula and then transported to East Malaysia.[22]

Another rather dubious instance suggested for further investigation by the Auditor-General was the sale of 11,517 pairs of ankle leather boots in good condition but no longer used by the Army. This was tendered together with twenty-nine types of minor motor vehicles spares. The Ministry of Defence received only one offer for all the items. The Tenders Board met and decided to accept the offer. But before this, the Tenders Opening Committee prepared the papers for consideration by the Tenders Board. The items to be disposed by the Army were entered into two pages of the tender forms. Twenty-two of the twenty-nine types of motor vehicles spares were identified in quantities. Seven types of spares were not identified in quantities. The boots were also not identified in quantities. Both these items not identified in quantities appeared on the second page.

The amazing thing was that the Tenders Board with incomplete information given by the Tenders Opening Committee, decided to accept the offer from the sole bidder. How much was the offer? RM120! A shock should have followed and caused a mental earthquake amongst members of the Tenders Board. The original cost of the 11,517 pairs of boots alone was about RM146,000. Forgetting the original cost of the twenty-nine types of motor vehicle spares, and just taking the cost of the boots, it meant that the sole bidder paid about 1.04 sen for each pair of boots. If we include the cost of the spares, that genius of a bidder must have paid minus one sen for each of the items.[23]

Amongst the irregularities noted by the Auditor-General was negligence in keeping records of navy stores to the point that it was impossible to ascertain whether items from the stores were properly issued. The lament of the Auditor-General applies here as it does to the irregularities concerning supply, when he said, 'Although I have for several years been reporting to ministries and departments and to the Treasury about the extent of irregularities in the supply of fresh rations, no action has to my knowledge been taken to stop such abuse as described in the preceding paragraphs, and this practice has cost and is continuing to cost the government several million dollars a year.'[24]

I have heard such laments of Auditor-Generals in Malaysia, for at least two decades. I believe the same applies to government auditors in other Asian countries. The auditors alone cannot do anything but expose the irregularities. From the Malaysian audit reports alone, there is sufficient grounds to suspect that corruption is firmly entrenched along the usual points of the decision-making chain in the administration where big expenditure is involved. But the situation in Malaysia is not as bad as in Indonesia, India and Pakistan. The tentacles of corruption have not seized the general public in the manner that they did in India and the other countries.

To illustrate how corruption enters the life of an individual to the extent that it becomes horridly oppressive, let us take the life history of an Indian in business, Mr Ram Narain.[25] We begin with his return from overseas. He paid the full custom duties on the articles he brought with him. However, on those he sent by sea, he asked a friend to clear them for him at Bombay and gave him Rs 4,000 for this purpose. The friend only spent Rs 500 and returned the rest to Mr Ram Narain. He was told that it was the prevailing practice at the port. As a result of the bribe, the goods were understated in value.

Mr Narain became a close confidant of a very rich businessman and industrialist and managed to arrange the use of all the man's cars, jeeps, trucks, manned by drivers, and provisioned with ample supplies of oil and petrol, for the political party of an influential minister in the state, at the minister's request. The same minister requested a generous contribution in Rs 10 notes, so that it would not be easy to trace. After this Ram Narain was involved with various negotiating activities for his firm involving bribes and services, one of which was to arrange for a minister and his family to stay for two months in one of the company's bungalows.

Then he had also to think of the various presents to key officials and their families on occasions such as weddings. After a while, Mr Narain became a lawyer and acted as a legal adviser for the sale of a house which was for Rs5 lakhs. He was asked to leave vacant the space for the price in the sale's deed. After registration the parties returned to pay Mr Narain's fees. The document recorded a sale of Rs 2 lakhs. The sub-registrar did the job with Rs 5,000.

From the law practice, Mr Narain moved to government service as a top official in the state government. One day he dismissed his domestic servant but was unable to make him vacate his quarters. He then filed a civil suit against the ex-servant, waited for several years, got a decree in his favour and tried to get it executed. Meanwhile, a message was conveyed to him that a goodwill fee for the ejecting official was expected. He paid Rs 200 for this.

Another much more serious incident happened to Mr Narain. His maid committed suicide by taking poison following ill treatment by her drunkard husband. He saw to it that a decent burial was given to her and in addition gave the husband Rs 500 for other expenses. A month later a police constable turned up and quietly informed him that he had committed an offence for not reporting the suicide. However, the entire episode would be hushed up if he would give Rs 500 to the sub-inspector of police. He paid the amount.

In a corrupt society, corruption enters into our lives at frequent intervals and at several intersections. The child is already exposed to its damaging effects while in primary school. Corruption becomes part of the visible scenery. An entire generation of children grow up under its shadow. What this would do to the personality of the individual is certainly something to worry about.

A general description of a corruption-ridden society is helpful, to enable us to sense the atmosphere and feel the gravity of the situation. An Indian observer said: 'Corruption is the largest single element to be found most in India. All roads, from the maternity hospital to the crematorium, smell of corruption. No individual is free from it, no area can be found where corruption is not a ritual.'[26]

Corruption becomes such a force that it conditions the socialization process of the younger generations towards a negative direction. Another observer described the Indian situation applicable to other corrupt countries. She said, 'In my opinion a nation whose young cannot find direction because nobody is capable of giving it is doomed. So they go no better in corrupt ways than their forbears. They have new techniques, a new loss of Indian innocence and a lack of religious feeling which aid them in this. Their ideal is total materialism, even when they profess communism or socialism and let all ideologies drown in sparkling glasses of scotch and whisky! The upper classes set this pattern and then follows the worker. Out of need, out of total lack of security he too becomes corrupt, even a petty thief.'[27]

THE CASE OF PAKISTAN

In Pakistan, the situation is much more odious because the corrupt pay lip service to religion. A Pakistani observer, appraising the ignominious state of his country, sadly stated that Islam in Pakistan is only in theory, in recitation, in prayers but not in the moral behaviour of the people. The influence of the leading classes, the hypocritical religious leaders, the scheming professionals, the greedy businessmen, the extortionist bureaucrats, have steadily increased the momentum of corruption. The accounts of corruption in Pakistan resemble those of India.

However, Pakistan is a state created anew during the partition period. As such it is easier to trace the changes in the intensity of corruption. In the beginning the amount of bribery was small and it concerned mostly lower-ranking government staff. But with the passage of time the course of bribery increased and close relations developed between the giver and receiver. They formed gangs and teams, cells and agencies to arrange their corrupt dealings. Government officials and businessmen developed ties of partnership. Large-scale transactions then started to take place. The services of touts and brokers came into being. In the early stages corruption was done in secrecy and shyness but later it was practised in broad daylight in government offices.[28]

As in India, corruption in Pakistan affects all walks of life. The courts, the revenue departments, the police, the health services, the railway, the customs, the telephone service, the postal service, the professional services, were all vigorously dominated by corruption of the most extortive type. Amongst the lawyers, corruption took the form of wrong advice, bribery of court and police officials, at times including judges and magistrates, and also the opponent's advocates. A common device was to entangle the clients into complications that cost them a lot of money.

In the medical profession, the manner was to squeeze as much money as possible from the patient. Specialists and surgeons attached to big hospitals prefer the patients to come to their private clinics first, settle their bills, and then they would be helped with admission into the hospitals. For operations, patients making such arrangements would get preferential treatment. Others had to wait days to get their turn.

In the education system, we have the familiar leakage of question papers. Examiners were bribed by students to obtain the required marks. In addition, some teachers forced tuition upon students and extracted loans from them. The religious teachers and leaders lacked moral character. They depended on gifts from the rich and corrupt. Some even advised their corrupt patrons that it was all right to juggle income-tax figures, to bribe and protect their rights. They declared that the government and its laws were un-Islamic and as such businessmen, as subjects of wrong and aggressive government, may juggle accounts, conceal their profit and wealth, and use bribes, to avert the unjust action of an erroneous government.[29]

The juggling was also applied to a person's age. The guardians of candidates appearing before examinations tampered with the candidates age so that they could remain within the age limits prescribed for entering government service. In other instances, the age was decreased so that one could stay longer in government service. All these recurring expressions of corruption made people lose confidence in the government and even the democratic system.

A religious scholar once suggested that election by popular vote should be prohibited and declared religiously unlawful (*haram*). On the premise that 80 to 90 per cent of the people were corrupt, invariably a candidate that stood for election would be corrupt. Thus election was for the corrupt, of the corrupt, and by the corrupt.[30] It was because of disgust towards corruption that the people and the Army initially welcomed the introduction of martial law in 1958.

An elaborate screening operation of government officials was afterwards carried out. But no sooner was this done when corruption returned in full force. The screening had the effect of preparing the soil for a more luxuriant growth. This was due to the fact that certain seeds with a great potential for survival passed the screening net and then vigorously regenerated themselves. As the corrupt officials were grouped together with those of integrity after they passed the screening, the corrupt acquired prestige and status. They further exploited their positions to bigger advantage. 'This explains the growing incidence of corrupt practices after a short lull during the early years of the first martial law administration.'[31]

Corruption in Pakistan has for a long time attained devastating magnitude. The misery and human suffering caused by corruption are beyond description. The state which was formed at great cost to human lives and suffering attending the partition tragedy, is now being abandoned by tens of thousands of its skilled and unskilled manpower. The brain as well as the brawn drain from Pakistan is truly impressive. This is one of the serious consequences of corruption which greatly affects the pace of development in the developing societies. The great harm corruption is doing to development is as clear as daylight. It does not require ingenuity and scholarship to recognize what is obvious. A very clear instance of the harmful effect of corruption to development is furnished by Indonesia. We shall single out for attention certain incidents, as the general condition in Indonesia is the same as in India and Pakistan.

THE CASE OF INDONESIA

In the first chapter of this book, I discussed some of the instances of corruption in Indonesia, many of which are similar to those of Pakistan and India.

The harm done by corruption towards development in Indonesia was highlighted by the Report of the Commission of Four, set up by order of President Suharto on 31 January 1970. The President himself dwelt upon the danger of corruption and the harm it could inflict on the state. Corruption, according to President Suharto, is immoral and obstructive to development. He said that corruption in Indonesia almost totally dominated the life of the nation and the state, particularly before 1966 (the Sukarno period).[32]

The Commission of Four was entrusted to advise the government on how to increase the effectiveness of the measures taken against corruption.[33] Between 18 and 25 July 1970, an Indonesian daily, *Sinar Harapan*, in Jakarta, published the reports of the Committee to the President, apparently before they were officially announced by the government. The daily took this action in the name of public interest.

We shall consider some of the observations made by the Commission on the government-owned oil enterprise Pertamina and some injurious activity in the logging industry. The Committee noted the corruption and inefficiency affecting Pertamina. It failed to resist foreign manipulation to push down the price of crude oil. Pertamina did not observe its obligation to transfer 55 per cent of its net profit to *Dana Pembangunan* (Development Fund). It paid its taxes according to its own assessment in amounts not reflective of its earnings. Contractual agreements entered into with foreign oil companies were not favourable to Pertamina. It appeared as though Pertamina was acting purely as a body to offer facilities to the foreign companies. In the clauses of the agreement on profit and production sharing, Pertamina was continuously linked with its obligations. The clauses on rights referred more to the foreign company. The obligations included assistance to obtain visas for the foreign personnel of the company.

The account books were to be surrendered to the foreign company. The purchase of materials to carry out the contractual exploitation was not in the hands of Pertamina. At the time of the report, Pertamina's area of operation was very extensive. It carried out oil production and marketing activities, as well as profit and production sharing with thirty-four other foreign oil companies. Amongst the irregularities committed by Pertamina was the non-payment of taxes. Between 1958 and 1963, Pertamina did not send in tax returns. In 1964, without submitting tax returns it paid Rp 35,855,500 tax. The same amount was paid in 1966. By 1967 the tax debt of Pertamina was Rp 1,344 billion.

It did not meet the obligation to the Development Fund, stated in its charter. For nine years, beginning in 1958, Pertamina did not contribute anything to the Development Fund. It contributed in 1964 and 1965. It was then estimated that its deficit for 1970 would be US$17 million. The Commission of Four found serious indications of corruption and irregularities. For instance Pertamina's internal auditor was also the contractor for the Pertamina hotels. It owed the government millions in taxes and other returns.

Next came the logging industry. In June 1970, 165 companies

were issued licences to log with a capital of US$106.65 million and Rp 285 million to cover an area of 9 million hectares. There was a logging boom then. The logging activity was not properly conducted. The Indonesian licence-holder would sell his rights for a fee of US$5 for each cubic metre of log to a foreign broker. This foreign broker would then contract his right to a third party who did the actual logging job. The original licence holder, whose gain was much smaller than his foreign contacts, did not pay the royalty and the licence fee. Hence, the government lost revenue from this source.

In addition to the above, the jungle was being destroyed by indiscriminate cutting and destructive practices. The Department of Agriculture then warned that 27 million hectares of jungle land was already destroyed and covered by wild grass. Irregularities and corruption found in the teak logging industry brought great losses to the government through cheating. The higher quality export timber was classified as local so that it could be sold cheaper. The wood was deliberately sawn in such a manner that it fell outside the export specification. The teak was also exported as logs thereby reducing government revenue. In short, despite the logging of high quality teak, officially the government received a lower quality production figure and sale amount. Both the buyer and the seller benefited from this deception.

We have seen the prevalence of corruption in some of the Asian countries. In the entire developing region of Asia, Singapore is the only government practically free of corruption. Thailand, the Philippines and Malaysia are facing the problem of corruption. Apart from Singapore, of all the developing countries of Asia, corruption is least pandemic in Malaysia. The fear is that it is growing. Since 1957, the year of independence, corruption has definitely been growing in Malaysia. We see numerous political figures and others amassing wealth through being in office. It is public knowledge that there is corruption going on in customs, the highway police, immigration, the courts, the land office, the supply acquisition units of the various ministries, the religious departments of the states of the federation, and the road transport offices.

Corruption in Malaysia has not reached the Indonesian and

Indian proportions to the degree of systemic malignancy. The daily needs of the public can still be obtained without corruption. The day-to-day business with any government authority can still be conducted without recourse to bribery for the vast majority of people. But bribery will come in at the level of business and special favours. The salary of government servants is sufficient at least for basic needs. In Thailand and Indonesia, the salary of government servants is not sufficient for the month. The insufficiency of salary induces low-level corruption. But the fact is that this very insufficiency is the effect of corruption. According to Admiral Sudomo, the former Minister of Manpower in the Indonesian Cabinet, the Indonesian government would be able to pay its civil servants sufficiently if taxes are properly collected.[34] The prevailing corruption caused the civil servants to receive salaries less than their requirement. Apparently the salary of civil servants is an indication of the degree to which corruption has rotted the body politic.

When corruption is very deep rooted and impresses the observer with its pervasiveness and assertive autonomy, the feeling is created that corruption has become a way of life. The next step is to try to excuse it, or even to justify it. I once heard in a conference the suggestion, from an Indonesian participant, to postpone the elimination of corruption.[35] The argument was that corruption helped to build a middle class. This middle class was believed to be the backbone of stability. Consequently he suggested to postpone, in the crucial phase of economic development, excessive action aimed at eliminating corruption.

The above view was put forward after about one decade of total systemic corruption in Indonesia. The well-known statesman and former vice-president and prime minister, the late Dr Mohammad Hatta, noted for his opposition to corruption, wrote in the 1950s that corruption had run riot through Indonesian society, infecting many government departments. Workers and government employees whose wages and salaries were insufficient for their daily needs were being exploited by corrupt elements. Businessmen with economic morality were pushed back. 'Bribery and graft have become increasingly common, to the detriment of our community and our country. Each year the government loses hundreds of millions rupiahs in duties and taxes which remain unpaid as a result of fraud and smuggling, both illegal and "legal".[36]

CORRUPTION AND THE HUMAN PERSONALITY

The prevalence of total systemic corruption has, as one of its effects, the weakening of the will to fight corruption. This weakening of the will manifests itself in various forms, such as resignation to the climate of corruption, attempts to relate it to preceding institutional and cultural norms, or to rapid development, or even to such things as the creation of a middle class. It is also generally accepted amongst those whose will is weakened that the repudiation of corruption is a Western trait. The writings of some Western scholars have contributed to this weakening of the will to fight corruption. They talk about corruption being functional to development.

The truth is the opposite. One of the most serious effects of corruption greatly affecting development is the brain drain. Corruption creates the conditions conducive to the brain drain in combination with other factors.

The dominant motivation of the brain drain is the sense of insecurity arising from an immoral social order, a corrupt environment, a decadent atmosphere, an indifferent dominant value system insensitive to professional self-esteem. The conditions generating this sense of insecurity act as a constant pressure operating under the climate of corruption. Lack of respect for constructive values among those in power and the general neglect and unconcern for the public good inevitably result in the emergence of conditions corrosive of security. The minority who are able to migrate are few but more find such conditions unbearable.

It would be helpful to learn of the vast majority trapped in the corrupt society under the most debilitating climate of corruption. How does corruption affect them psychologically and individually. What does corruption do to the human personality? It was in 1952, in Tehran, that I first became interested in the effects of corruption. At that time corruption was rampant. Government servants had not been paid their salaries for months and months. Yet the high officials went around with big cars, owned houses and entertained themselves outside.

Subsequently, I visited Indonesia where corruption had also taken root. I became interested in knowing its effect on the personality of the victim as well as the perpetrator. A distinction has to be made here between a victim and a partner of corruption. When a businessman willingly bribes a government official to accomplish a sales transaction, he becomes a partner of corruption. When a citizen has to bribe to acquire a passport, he becomes a victim of corruption. The passport is his right for which he has to pay illegally. There is no question of favoured treatment here. There is no question of his taking away other people's rights. The injustice committed is solely against himself, not against others. He becomes a victim of extortion.

It is the effect of this extortive corruption that tells on the personality, particularly if you have to go through life passing successive points of extortive corruption. The first effect is the rise of a pessimistic attitude. The future is full of uncertainty. The law and ethical norms are not there to protect the individual. Honesty, hard work and self-development do not help to increase happiness, security and welfare. After going through a few years of such an experience, the surrounding corruption becomes a phenomenon like the climate, something abiding and beyond human ability to change. When this mood spreads among the population, the people become passive and inert. They accept a life dominated by evil.

Gradually their feelings become insensitive to virtuous ideals. Their social conscience is numbed. There is loss of faith in moral ideals and government. People accept government as an unavoidable evil from which not much good can be expected.

Within this setting there is usually a small minority that rejects corruption and feels that it is against human dignity. Against this minority the advocates of corruption never cease to labour. They try insidiously to make people accept corruption and to belittle the moral ideal. They say corruption is an Asian way of life. The impersonal and efficient concept of bureaucracy is a Western import. The distinction between public and private interest is a Western attitude foreign to the Asian mind.

Anything from the cultural tradition of their society would be manipulated to suit the interest of corruption. It was suggested that the gift offered to officials in Asian societies of the past was never considered objectionable. What happens now is only a continuation of this practice of the past. However, one thing was forgotten. In the past, side by side with the gift, there was also such a thing as corruption. The ancient Asians made a distinction between the gift regulated by custom and corruption. There was such a thing as bribing judges in ancient times.

The gift which was publicly given was often reciprocated by the recipient. It was not done in a clandestine manner. It was not intended to injure the rights of others. It was not the same as bribery. I had seen this happening many times in Java during my childhood days. The secret advocates of corruption intended to make the people consider corruption as an Asian way of life by pointing to the institution of the gift as its foundation.

One of the most devastating effects of corruption is the chronic inefficiency and bureaucratic personalization. It was suggested with the blessing of some sociologists and political scientists that Asia knew no impersonal and achievement-oriented bureaucracy in the past. The modern bureaucracy and its impersonal norms are said to be a creation of the West. This suggestion is based on complete ignorance of Asian history. How many times did the Chinese sages advise the emperor not to go to his nephew, but to the tailor in order to make a suit? Indeed no emperor was known to have preferred his nephew to occupy the post of general in the army above a proven warrior.

The norms of efficiency and impersonal rule were present in Asian history. They were often violated in the areas the ruling classes considered not crucial to the maintenance of their power. Even a tyrant would not appoint his father-in-law head of the secret police if he was stupid. He would appoint his father-in-law as lord of a lucrative province. There are countless instances showing that the norms of integrity and efficiency belong to the general Asian tradition. The teachings of Hindu, Buddhist, Islamic and Chinese sages are excellent sources of the anti-corruption outlook.

In the attempt to differentiate between Western and Asian

tradition some observers have drawn the line too far. Some have gone to the extent of creating a picture which has no existence in real life. One such picture was drawn by Bronowski of the Japanese. He had a very unusual impression of the Japanese. According to him the Japanese would never understand why anyone would want to know of anything. The Easterner is a person who has no interest in fact. Bronowski's judgement is so unbelievable that it serves us well to cite him. He said: 'The cultures of the East still differ from ours as they did then. They still belittle man as individual man. Under this runs an indifference to the world of the senses, of which the indifference to experienced fact is one face. Anyone who has worked in the East knows how hard it is there to get an answer to a question of fact. When I had to study the casualties from the atomic bomb in Japan at the end of the war, I was dogged and perplexed by this difficulty. The man I asked, whatever man one asks, does not really understand what one wants to know; or rather, he does not understand that one wants to know. He wants to do what is fitting, he is not unwilling to be candid, but at bottom he does not know the facts because they are not his language. These cultures of the East have remained fixed because they lack the language and the very habit of fact.'[37]

That Asian culture belittles the individual, that it is indifferent to the world of facts, that it does not value the effort to understand, is part of the general stereotyping of the non-Western world by those who should have known better. This misunderstanding has also affected the perception of corruption by Asian culture. It was also suggested that the Asians have a different sense of public morality. What was missed is the fact that the prevalence of corruption and maladministration in Asian societies was a violation of the norms rather than an expression of them. When it comes to Western societies as early as those of ancient Greece, the prevalence of corruption was considered a violation of the norms.

It is not possible in this book to present the teachings of Asian sages and thinkers against corruption. I am confining myself here to the theme of corruption and its effects on the human personality. There are many kinds of effects on the personality, one of which is the sense of powerlessness and self-abasement. In 1975 my wife visited India, a country with a proud and glorious tradition. She accompanied a friend to a hospital to visit someone there. In the waiting room she overheard an animated discussion between a doctor and a man who wanted to admit his wife on account of a mental breakdown. My wife understood the language spoken. The man was agitated because the doctor insisted on a bribe in order to admit his wife. Finally the man agreed after haggling about the amount.

Let us imagine ourselves to be in such a situation. How would we feel? We become the object of a cruel and overpowering exploitation. We are in the most dependent condition, in need of help. Yet what we get is a cruel exploitation. We have to accept it for there is no other way out. The sense of disgust, anger, disillusionment, injustice, inflicted cruelty and abasement for having to give in, whirl within us but yet there is no possible outlet of expression. The suppression of our inner frustration and anger at the surrounding injustice affecting us will inflict psychological as well as somatic wounds on our person. This probably explains the fact that there is such a high incidence of hypertension in very corrupt societies.

The most alarming fact is the ease with which the personality is converted into the destructive type. It is a law of life that it is easier to destroy than to build. It is easier to destroy a personality than to build one. The most pernicious influence of corruption is the fact that it also makes its victims depraved. They become part of the system. If they later hold positions of power they themselves abuse it. There are many of the younger generation who, growing up in a corrupt society, become corrupt themselves after being subjected to extortive corruption during their school days.

This is a psychological truth. If ten children were subjected to cruel treatment at home, most would be cruel later to their children. Only a few would not. The biggest problem in a corrupt society is that the system inducts by far a greater number than it repels. Hence the prospect of changing it becomes more and more remote. The grave crisis in corruption-ridden Asian societies is truly the absence of the correct human type.

The problem of the correct human type transcends the problem of ideology, cliques or political policies. Before anything else you need an honest man. No matter which ideology, which clique or which policy prevails, as long as the human type expressing it is corrupt, the problem will remain. That is the reason why it is difficult to change a corrupt society within half a century despite political changes of the ruling groups. On the contrary, the half a century may be taken up by the further growth of corruption as clearly indicated in many Asian countries. The thirty-five years that have elapsed since World War II in the Asian region are characterized by a vigorous growth of corruption.

This growth is further abetted by the prolific multiplication of the corrupt human type occupying positions of power and authority. The ruling power breeds its own type. If you have the negative type in the beginning they will multiply like rabbits. Once this takes place it will be very difficult to change except through a successful revolution dominated by the right moral type. Even a successful revolution would have great difficulties in keeping corruption under control. In the very process, the corrupt human type, which was earlier deprived of the opportunity to exploit power, would do the utmost to gain control.

Finally, I would like to bring the reader's attention to an observation in the final report of the Bumiputra Malaysia Finance Committee of Enquiry on the problem of the Bumiputra Malaysia Finance (BMF) loans scandal. The case of the BMF—in which the greed and perfidy of a few individuals, with their deceit, fraud and subterfuges, managed to siphon RM2.5 billion (US$1.02 billion) through dubious loans from a single institution, the BMF, through the Carrian Group in Hong Kong—is well known throughout the world. I believe there is nothing comparable to it in the annals of corruption. The government White Paper on this affair highlighted the fraud and malpractices that started in 1979 and ended in 1982. In January 1984, the Prime Minister of Malaysia named a three-man committee of enquiry following allegations that an estimated US$1.02 billion, given as loans to the Carrian Group in Hong Kong, involved the payment of some consultancy fees to some members of the board of directors of BMF's parent company, Bank Bumiputra Malaysia Berhad.[38]

The entire BMF Report deserves special study. Here I would like to highlight one of the committee's significant observations, that laws alone are not sufficient to guarantee a healthy and proper climate and public confidence. The law requires a complementary human type to enforce it in line with its spirit. The committee in its report emphasizes that legal controls in themselves are not sufficient. The personal quality and integrity of those entrusted with management are even more important.[39]

This point is highlighted in the first chapter of this book, first published in 1968, that rational and efficient laws alone are not enough to prevent the onslaught of corruption. In the last analysis, the successful prevention of corruption requires office-holders of high moral calibre. Neither can be without the other. This has been forcefully presented by Wang An Shih, the great Chinese Prime Minister and reformer of the eleventh century.[40]

Endnotes

1. *Report of the Committee on the Prevention of Corruption*, Ministry of Home Affairs, Government of India, New Delhi, n.d., p. 6.

2. *Ibid.*, pp. 6–7.

3. *Ibid.*, pp. 7–8.

4. *Ibid.*, pp. 9–10.

5. *Ibid.*, p. 10.

6. *Ibid.*, pp. 11–12.

7. *Ibid.*, p. 12.

8. *Ibid.*, p. 200.

9. *SADACHAR—Movement for Purity in National Life*, Ministry of Information and Broadcasting, Government of India, New Delhi, 1964, p. 5.

10. Suresh Kohli (ed.), *Corruption in India*, Chetana Publications, New Delhi, 1978, p. 43: In the art of Inder Maholtra.

11. *Ibid.*, p. 87. From the contribution of Dev Dut.

12. *Ibid.*

13. *Ibid.*, p. 88. Dev Dut's chapter, 'In Politics'.

14. *Ibid.*, see the contribution of Balraj Mehta, 'Black Market: Black Money'.

15. *Ibid.*, pp. 110–11. From the contribution of Usha Rai.

16. *Ibid.*, p. 111.

17. *Ibid.*, p. 114.

18. M. A. Azam, *The Anatomy of Corruption*, Society for Pakistan Studies, Dacca, 1970, p. 7.

19. Narendra K. Singhi, *Bureaucracy: Positions and Persons*, Abhinav Publications, New Delhi, 1974, p. 205.

20. *Ibid.*, p. 207.

21. M. Halayya, *Emergency: A War on Corruption*, S. Chand, New Delhi, 1978, p. 40.

22. *Report of the Auditor-General, Federal Government, Malaysia, 1977*, Kuala Lumpur, 1980, p. 124.

23. On this see *ibid.*, p. 126. All this was done by the civilian branch of the Defence Ministry.

24. *Ibid.*, p. 125.

25. The name is fictitious but the instances are based on true happenings. This account is from M. Halayya, *op. cit.*, pp. 61–8. It is presumably derived from K. N. Subramaniam, 'The Many Faces of Corruption', *The Economic Times*, Bombay, 2 September 1973, cited in the footnote.

26. In Suresh Kohli, *op. cit.*, p. 67. From the contribution of Chatana Kholi.

27. *Ibid.*, p. 105. From the contribution of Vimla Patil.

28. A. Rashid, *Corruption in Pakistan*, 1965, pp. 2–3. This small booklet was published apparently by the author himself. Though he seemed not to be familiar with the English language, many ideas he tried to express are interesting and reflective of the problems around him.

29. *Ibid.*, p. 24.

30. M. A. Azam, *op. cit.*, p. 19.

31. *Ibid.*, p. 6. Members of the new ruling clique were also actively corrupt.

32. *Amanat Presiden Soeharto dalam Sidang Kabinet Paripurna 31 Djanuari 1970, Djakarta*, Departmen Penerangan Republik Indonesia, Djakarta, 1970.

33. The Committee members were S. H. Wilopo (Chairman), I. J. Kasimo, Prof. Ir. Johannes and A. Tjokroaminoto. The adviser was former Vice-President Dr Mohammad Hatta.

34. This was told to me in a meeting with him at his office in Jakarta on 24 August 1982.

35. International Conference on Southeast Asian Studies, 23–26 February 1972, University of Malaya, Kuala Lumpur.

36. Mohammad Hatta, *The Co-operative Movement in Indonesia*, Cornell University Press, Ithaca, 1957, pp. 84–5.

37. J. Bronowski, *Science and Human Values*, Julian Messner, New York, 1956, pp. 57–8.

38. On this scandal, see Appendix A.

39. See Appendix B. For the source, see BMF *Committee of Enquiry Final Report*, Bank Bumiputra Malaysia Berhad, Kuala Lumpur, 1986, vol. 2, p. 942.

40. See 4 and 5 of this book.

Chapter 3

THE STRUGGLE AGAINST CORRUPTION

S INCE 1957, corruption has steadily increased in Malaysia and also the rest of the ASEAN (Association of Southeast Asian Nations) countries, with the exception of Singapore. There are clearly identifiable reasons why corruption has not taken root in Singapore. Of course, the social, economic and historical conditions of Singapore differ greatly from those of the other ASEAN countries. It has been suggested that the small size of Singapore has made it easier to control the problem of corruption. But this is only partially true. Other small island states are known to be corrupt. Before the present regime came to power, there was a lot of corruption in Singapore going back to earlier decades.

The point to remember is that throughout the Third World there has been a prolific increase in corruption since World War II when most of the countries in the Afro-Asian region attained independence. Thirty years have elapsed since the first edition of this book was published. The general theoretical framework of corruption presented then still remains valid. New and more complex cases of corruption have emerged. The BMF affair serve only to confirm the observation made by Wang An Shih and others before him.

There have been comments and references made in the Indonesian press to the issues relating to the stages of corruption raised in the previous edition of this book, which has seen two Indonesian and one Japanese translation. It is felt that Indonesia is approaching the last stage when corruption becomes self-destructive; when the corrupt themselves find corruption a problem. When you acquire wealth through corruption and invest it in business, you do not want that business to be threatened by corruption. It is known that American crime bosses are increasingly investing in legitimate and clean businesses because of the security it provides. I did not believe then Indonesia had reached the stage during the 1980s that a strong resistance to corruption to the point of becoming a great political force would emerge. However, recent events have shown that reaction against corruption have become more open and forceful.

For Third World countries, corruption will remain the number one problem for a long time to come. It is necessary to awaken public awareness to the danger posed by corruption. The phenomenon has to be studied from all angles. Justice Sardar Muhammad Iqbal, the Federal Ombudsman of Pakistan, has called for a crusade against corruption by every member of society.[1] The problem of corruption is being felt more and more. The editorial of a Pakistani weekly reflects the mood and desperation of those against corruption. It quotes Prime Minister Mohammad Khan Junejo who has repeatedly said that corruption is a deep-rooted disease requiring determined efforts on the part of the government to combat it. The issue has been debated in the Pakistan National Assembly. Some organizational apparatus have been set up. The various solutions suggested to overcome the problem reveals the confusion and inadequate knowledge of the nature of corruption.

It is useful to quote in full what the editorial says on this matter. Commenting on the setting up of organizational apparatus to combat corruption, it says: 'But beyond that it is hard to find any ray of light at the end of the tunnel. Each elected member has a panacea of his own. The so-called religious lobby vigorously advances the theory that hastening the process of Islamization would end it once and for all. Another group, to which the Minister of Finance also belongs, believes that in decentralization of powers and deregulation of procedures lies the real answer. Still others claim, somewhat naively perhaps, that enforcement of simple living among public servants would discourage the get-rich-quick trend and a system of proper accountability would finish it and so on. There is nothing wrong with all these ideas except that their efficacy has always been in doubt. The process of Islamization has been tried, and tried under martial law, and it has had little effect.

In fact, it has sometimes been alleged that the machinery of martial law itself has been tainted by it. The proposal of decentralization and deregulation, despite having been discussed for months, is nowhere near materialization. The public servants dealing with contracts, permissions, permits, etc., are not likely to part with their powers without a fight and, if forced to give them up, are not expected to become saints overnight. Other ways to feather their nests are likely to be found. The campaign for simple living, first thought of and promoted during the early Ayub Khan days, soon came to an ignominious end.'[2]

The attempt to wipe out corruption is not a simple drawing up of a programme of action. It is a fight against the corrupt, clinging to their position, subverting measures against corruption. It is a struggle for survival of two contending groups, the corrupt and those against it, in a manner of jungle warfare in the dark, where the enemy is not seen but nevertheless is fighting back with all its might.

Again let us hear the editorial: 'The task gets complicated by other factors, some of them actually indicative of lack of sincerity in certain seats of power. One should, for example, try to find out why the provinces have avoided the appointment of their own Ombudsmen. Surely, it poses no administrative problem to them. The only answer that appears plausible is that they do not want their administrative machinery to come under the scrutiny of an impartial body. Then again, it would be of interest to note why the streamlining of the revenue and police departments is resisted. Does the answer lie in the fact that both these institutions are used for political ends and any diminution of their authority would reduce their usefulness as political tools? Even more disconcerting are rumours that some of the elected representatives themselves are not above corruption. They, it is alleged, undertake to help supplicants for a price. One hopes that such rumours are without any basis but, if true, from where does one begin the process of reform? Determination to root out corruption is one thing and to find the means to do so is another. But a few things are obvious. The FIA and the anti-corruption cells and wings and departments have been tried again and again and, for various reasons, have been found wanting. It would not serve any purpose to harness them again to the task. This does not, however, mean that there is no way out of the dilemma. Some suggestions, including those offered in these columns on many occasions earlier, are worth trying. But, apart from that, much more than a sound resolve is required. It requires a lot of courage—courage to probe even one's friends and colleagues. No one is likely to believe such resolutions unless the process starts right from the top.'[3]

The development of corruption in Pakistan reflects what is going on in the rest of the Third World countries. As corruption increases, more and more pronouncements are made against it with not much effect. During his tenure, President Zia of Pakistan publicly acknowledged the incidence of corruption in Pakistan society, and expressed his determination to root it out. In one of his later speeches, he reluctantly admitted that his efforts had met with less than success.[4] Among the measures he attempted was to orientate public functionaries to a sense of rectitude by encouraging prayers and spiritual cleansing of the soul, which, it was hoped, would improve the behaviour of public servants.

The editorial of the weekly earlier cited observes the following: 'But as of now there is no sign of this cancer responding to the treatment. If anything, it seems to be spreading even further. It is not easy after all to change the morals of the people with just the message of the truth. The Prophet Noah could not bring even all the members of his family to the path ordained by God. And Christ, despite all the miracles at his command, won only twelve disciples to his cause during his lifetime. So if one has any doubts about the efficacy of the measures aimed at moral reformation of our society, one should not immediately be dubbed as being anti-religious and a pessimist. But luckily the crusade that the President launched was not confined to a programme of moral reformation alone. He ordered anti-corruption cells to be set up in each government department. He promised stringent punishments for the guilty. He appointed a *Wafaqi Mohtasib* at the federal level, etc. But except for some limited success achieved by the *Wafaqi Mohtasib*—limited because he was given only limited powers (fairly large areas being placed outside his jurisdiction—nothing else seemed to have worked). So it is quite understandable that when Prime

Minister Mohammad Khan Junejo took up office, among the very first tasks that he assigned himself was the eradication of corruption. He has not had time, of course, to chalk out a programme of action yet. And it would be unwise to venture a guess about the prospects of his success, but the point to be noted is that he deems it to be a major national problem.'5

Then the National Assembly of Pakistan decided to debate the issue. Again it was observed: 'But one thing is apparent—no one has so far stood up and claimed that the official machinery is not completely rotten. In fact, everyone seemed to agree that even those areas of the public sector which were relatively free from corruption in the past, such as those of education, had now been afflicted by it. The most notorious agency was, of course, said to be the police.'6

Some months later, in March 1986, reacting to the news that a committee was to be formed to determine the causes of corruption and make recommendations to the Cabinet, the weekly listed several types of corruption, one of which is what we have called the extortive type. 'The police, certain categories of our judicial machinery and lower level employees in the land revenue department fall into this class. Among these functionaries the police have the further advantage of extorting money from even those who may not be a party to any dispute. Threat to involve an innocent person in criminal cases does the trick. In such deals between the givers and takers of bribes, although the victims of injustice are apparently the only sufferers, in a broader perspective, it is the reputation of the government that suffers.'7

The preventive measures which have been earlier tried and thought about apparently were not effective. We shall again quote the weekly, for it summarizes the general difficulty found elsewhere in Third World countries. The editorial says: 'There are no universal cures. It has been suggested that had punishment for a corrupt official been made more stringent than just a simple dismissal from service, he would have mended his ways. Confiscation of property and imprisonment of the guilty has been suggested quite often. There may be some merit in this but it does not tell us how to catch the corrupt. There are whole departments riddled with corruption. How should the guilty in such departments be caught when everyone is a party to it and would do everything to protect the others? Divesting them of personal discretion, dismantling of controls, use of automatic computers and other modern machines for evaluation of works and receipts and payment of public funds have also been suggested before, though never tried. The least effective has been the so-called social and moral reformation campaign conducted with a lot of fanfare during the past ten years. And although this has again been proposed on the floor of the National Assembly, the chances of its success are virtually nil. Idealism may have some value for the idealistically inclined but is of little use to the hard-boiled cynics who constitute the majority of the corrupt. In the end, we would like to suggest that if serious headway towards the containment of this evil in our society is to be made then one should not set about covering the same ground which has been covered again and again since the days of Ayub Khan.'[8]

AN OMBUDSMAN'S EXPERIENCE

The practical difficulty surrounding the effort to get rid of corruption is enormous. It comes from all sides. The biggest is the obstacles arising from a corrupt and inefficient bureaucracy. Any effort to correct injustice and reduce the suffering of the victims should be attempted however limited its success may be. The experience itself is valuable and revealing. An example is the institution of Ombudsman in Pakistan which began in August 1983. *Wafaqi Mohtasib* Sardar Iqbal recounted some of his illuminating experiences in his annual report for 1984.

In 1984, he received 38,030 complaints. During the year, positive redress was provided in 2,048 cases while complaints dismissed were 1,942 and the rest under investigation. 'Some notable cases are also briefly mentioned in the report. Compensation of Rs. 5.5 million paid to landowners of Attock, whose land was acquired many years ago. Sale of rotten government wheat stopped to prevent human consumption. Financial compensation paid to a public servant for the mental torture suffered by him. Many insurance policies withheld by PLI paid to policy-holders. Multan landowner paid compensation after 13 years. *Zakat* ensured to 100 poor persons who went without stipends for five months. Millions of rupees, disputed by National Savings and nationalised banks, credited to account holders. Electricity restored to a mosque after two years. Telephone connection given after 24 years. Long delayed compensation of Rs. 15 million to landowners in NWFP. Discontinued express train resumed on public demand. Action against corrupt officials of Pakistan Steel Mill. Million of rupees paid in pending rebates and refunds in customs duty and income tax. Restoration of a public servant's pension after 19 years etc. etc.'[9]

In a sea of corruption, the above may appear like drops of rain but the multiplying effect is more than what is shown by the figures. Justice Sardar Iqbal's meetings with complainants was a moving experience. Never in his life had he come across so much suffering and distress.[10] At least the institution of the Ombudsman could provide some hope, however small it might be, for the struggle against corruption. We know that a successful struggle against corruption depends more than anything else on the will of the ruling class. In its absence, the public has to generate the pressure. The institution of the Ombudsman can help to do precisely this, to awaken public morale which has been hitherto suppressed by innumerable obstructions.

A most significant obstruction is a corrupt and servile press. What the press can do is tremendous. Justice Sardar Iqbal paid his heartfelt tribute to the press for its support and for publicizing his decisions. This, he said, had aroused the public and made it aware of its administrative rights and the bureaucracy to feel accountable to the public. However, there are various other obstructions such as a lack of financial and personnel resources. Another obstruction has been noted earlier, that of the unwillingness of the provinces to introduce the institution of Ombudsman.

In his 1983 report, Justice Sardar Iqbal revealed that 50 per cent of the complaints came from provincial sources. The excesses and corrupt practices of provincial authorities required the urgent attention of the Ombudsman as much as those of the federal. Yet the jurisdiction of the Ombudsman was limited to the federal agencies. 'It is tragic to contemplate that almost 3,900 citizens aggrieved at the hands of the provincial bureaucracies have stayed without any relief from the Ombudsman because he had no jurisdiction to look into their cases. It

85

is tragic also to contemplate that complaints against provincial agencies have continued to pour into the *Mohtasib's* office in spite of repeated reminders to the contrary.'[11]

At the time of writing this book, I do not know whether this strange situation has been rectified. It definitely weakens the attempt to eliminate corruption. A very fertile source of corruption, bureaucratic delay and inefficiency, which has been mentioned in the first chapter of this book, was widely prevalent in the provinces. Justice Sardar Iqbal sees bureaucratic delay as a serious problem encouraging corruption.

Another very serious impediment in the fight against corruption is public hesitation to come forward. As Justice Sardar Iqbal observes: 'There is no dearth of talk about corruption which, no doubt, exists. However, it may be noted that the real victim of corruption is often the government itself. Both the corrupter and the corrupted benefit from this nefarious practice. Understandably the beneficiaries are reluctant to lodge complaints which partly explains that only a small number of concrete complaints have been made about corruption. It would be interesting to observe that in the majority of cases where allegations of corruption have been levelled, we have not been receiving any reply on return call for confirmation.'[12]

But this hesitation to come forward is often the case when the forces of corruption are still dominant and all pervasive. Added to this is the dampening of morale by the leniency of court judgments against the corrupt. A case in hand is that of a minor functionary in the office of the Deputy Commissioner, Lahore, found guilty of taking bribes and sentenced to two years of rigorous imprisonment by a trial magistrate. This sentence was reduced to two months by the High Court in answer to an appeal by him. Not satisfied with this, the defendant appealed to the Supreme Court against the conviction. The Supreme Court upheld the conviction and in its concluding observation stressed the need to deal with corruption with an iron hand. It pointed out that the common man was hesitant to report cases of extortion for fear of reprisal and involvement in litigation. When he took the risk of reporting, he discovered that the punishment given was light and this had the effect of inducing corrupt officials to continue with their practice.

The editor of the weekly cited earlier has this to say: 'The Supreme Court's observations underline a problem that has not received much attention in our society. There are myriad causes of flourishing corruption in our midst, but an important one is that the punishment is seldom commensurate with the enormity of the crime. Given the wide powers enjoyed by all levels of bureaucracy, it is not easy for an ordinary citizen to take the risk of reporting cases of extortion to the concerned authorities. But even where such cases are reported, the convict is able to get away lightly and resumes his evil trade. Inadequate and half-hearted punishment acts as a direct encouragement to others of his ilk. The situation calls for corrective action at two levels. One, the punishment for those found indulging in graft should be stiffened and made really deterrent and two, courts should show no leniency to the corrupt and should award them the maximum punishment permissible under the law. Once the corrupt get to know that the punishment their misdemeanor will attract is harsh and that it will be applied with full force if they are found out, they are sure to pause in their tracks. The society cannot get rid of corruption unless it goes about tackling the problem with the severity it deserves.'[13]

The hesitation of aggrieved parties to come forward can be better understood within the context of the prevailing psychological climate. In a highly corrupt society, the prevailing climate of authority is characterized by negligence, indifference, inefficiency, decadence and corruption. These phenomena form a cluster, the mainspring of which is corruption. A generation which has been brought up under this climate is more inclined to tolerate it rather than to resist it. Short of a revolution, only the determination of the ruling class can effectively change this climate. What if the ruling class itself is corrupt or permissive of corruption?

In such a situation, the driving force is what I suggest we call 'collective outrage'. The editorial of a well-known Indonesian daily, *Kompas*, commented on this suggestion and stressed the need for the entire society to develop a sense of shame and outrage with regard to injustice, corruption, negligence and inefficiency.[14] If there is such a strong public opinion, an indifferent ruling class would be compelled to take notice of it and gradually imbibe it itself. At this stage of Asian history, the propagation of collective shame and outrage is crucial. The weakening of the sense of outrage is the effect of corruption.

THE BMF SCANDAL

The absence of a forceful nation-wide outrage is clearly evident in the affairs surrounding the BMF scandal, noted earlier. The circumstances to elicit a sense of outrage are there. The whole affair was so clearly fraudulent and crude that it would have easily awakened the sense of outrage. The Malaysian Prime Minister, Dr Mahathir Mohamad, called the BMF affair a betrayal of trust and a heinous crime.[15] There are two aspects of the scandal that should awaken tidal outrage amongst the Malaysian public, as opposed to the mere reaction of the press and some politicians. One is the act itself, the RM2.5 billion scandal, and the other is the attitude towards the major participants of the scandal.[16]

The BMF Committee of Enquiry headed by Auditor-General Tan Sri Ahmad Noordin Zakaria describes the situation as follows: 'In our enquiry, we have come across several instances of irregularities, frauds, criminal breach of trust, theft, actions in complete disregard of honest commercial practice and contravention of several laws, in Malaysia and in Hong Kong, in respect of the administration and operations of BMF.'[17] The Report urges criminal proceedings to be taken against certain persons involved, including those in the parent company, Bank Bumiputra Malaysia Berhad.[18] The Report recommends three special briefs to be submitted to the police in Kuala Lumpur and Hong Kong for further investigations. One of them, the first, has not been submitted to the police in Kuala Lumpur. The Hong Kong authorities have actively investigated the matters reported to them.[19]

On 7 May 1985, the Report suggests that criminal investigation be started by the Attorney-General and a police report lodged on the first series of loans amounting to US$292 million given by BMF (Hong Kong) to Plessey Investment Limited, a Hong Kong company with a paid-up capital of HK$2. The withdrawal and use of this amount, in the Report's view, is tantamount to theft.[20] A similar suggestion was made on 20 November 1986, referring to additional cases of fraud.[21] On 8 December 1985, the same suggestion was made regarding yet other cases.[22]

However, these cases could have been unravelled earlier. An inspection team from *Bank Negara* (State Bank) submitted its report on BMF (Hong Kong) on 30 September 1982. Here it listed certain unsatisfactory features in the operations of BMF.[23] There was very heavy lending to two groups, the Carrian (HK$3.246 billion) and the Kevin Hsu (HK$0.755 billion), totalling HK$4.001 billion. This was 79.4 per cent of the entire loan portfolio of BMF then, which was HK$5.042 billion. This was definitely dangerous and undesirable.

It pointed out that the beneficial ownership of the Carrian Group was not entirely known. BMF (Hong Kong) showed it very special treatment with undesirable features, including window dressing of accounts. As a result of this special relationship, BMF liberally made available loans and advances amounting to HK$3.246 billion as at 30 June 1982. The bulk of these was granted on an unsecured basis. Then there was the mention of payments of consultancy fees to the directors of BMF and to the group chairman of BBMB in Kuala Lumpur. The enormity of the loans, the relaxed terms and lack of security, the consultancy fees, the window dressing of accounts, were all there. It should have made those with superior authority and responsibility burst with rage against such doubtful loans and start drastic action against the corrupt and manipulative elements. However, no such reaction has taken place.

Until now, no one has been criminally prosecuted despite the Report's insistence that a crime has been committed. This is not the case in Hong Kong. However, four former BMF (Hong Kong) officials — the chairman, two directors and the general manager—were sued in Kuala Lumpur by BBMB and BMF on 10 January 1985. The companies claimed damages of US$17.5 million, which they alleged were loaned to two Carrian companies. According to BBMB and BMF, the four had by 'their own neglect, want to skill or misconduct in management' caused the bank and BMF to suffer damage or loss of US$47.5 million.[24] They were not criminally prosecuted. No warrant of arrest has been issued for any of them.

The strange thing is that the government's White Paper, cited earlier, lists the above affair under criminal action in Malaysia (*Tindakan Jenayah di Malaysia*).[25] Why it appears in court as a civil suit requires explanation but the White Paper is silent on this. On the contrary, the White Paper appears to distantiate itself from the Report. The impression is given that the White Paper is merely presenting the views of the Report without committing itself to these views. The presentation is done in the interest of the Prime Minister, the Deputy Prime Minister and the Minister of Trade and Industry and one or two others who needed to clarify certain matters connected with their being mentioned in the Report.

The above impression is derived from the use of inverted commas in the White Paper when referring to the words 'prima facie'.[26] The reference to prima facie cases of corruption in the White Paper differs from similar references in the Report in the sense that the White Paper puts the words 'prima facie' within inverted commas, implying that it leaves the question open whether it is prima facie or otherwise. The White Paper notes five reports for criminal action lodged by BBMB in Kuala Lumpur, three of which were in 1984. Dates for the other two are not mentioned. It is possible that the government does not want to prejudge the issue, leaving it to the court to decide, but it has not been brought to court as a criminal offence. If the White Paper merely wants to present the Report as it is for the purpose of clarification, then the inverted commas should not be there since at any rate the term 'prima facie' is the suggestion of the Report, not the White Paper.

The BMF scandal is indeed a most alarming and revealing scandal. On 1 February 1986, at the National Front Youth Seminar on Politics, in Morib, Selangor, I suggested that Parliament should request the King to declare the BMF scandal a National Disaster (*Bencana Negara*).[27] It is not only the loss of RM2.5 billion that is the issue here but the surrounding phenomena of decadence, indifference, inattentiveness, the absence of communication, and most alarming, the freedom exercised by the corrupt manipulators to operate at such a scale and for so long, a couple of years, with boldness and minimal intelligence. The things they did as revealed by the Report does not show much intelligence. It is not a highly sophisticated scheme to defraud, nor is it difficult to detect or prove. It is a crude and rapacious manipulation leaving traces all over the place.

The question is how such a crude and unsophisticated fraud such a great scale could have been executed with all the freedom to the point that the Prime Minister then, was not aware of it. After the exposure of the BMF scandal, he became, together with many others, very incensed by the whole affair. His remarks about the parent company BBMB drew great attention. BBMB's lending policies (referring to the years before 1985), according to him, were just as bad as those of the BMF. As adviser to Petronas, the national oil company that bailed BBMB out, he was concerned about its domestic bad loans amounting to millions of ringgit. As a majority shareholder of BBMB, Petronas was interested in cleaning up BBMB through its new board of directors. He said: 'It is a standing joke in town that anyone who wants to become a millionaire can go to BBMB.'[28] He referred to malpractices by some of the bank officials.

It is clear from the above disclosure that the BMF scandal is only an exaggerated version of what has been going on in the parent company, the BBMB. The response to the scandal is interesting. While generally there is agreement that the culprits should be punished, there is a divergence of views as to how this should be done. Pronouncements from government circles have the tendency to create public anxiety and a sense of insecurity. A Royal Commission of Enquiry with powers to call witnesses was suggested by the leader of the opposition party, Mr Lim Kit Siang, and others, notably Tun Hussein Onn.

The government did not agree to setting up such a commission of enquiry. The Prime Minister, Dr Mahathir Mohamad, said that such a commission would be restricted in jurisdiction and could not have covered Hong Kong. Hence he preferred instead and internal committee of enquiry from the parent body, the BBMB.[29] However, the committee did not have the power to summon witnesses and compel them to answer as would have been the case with a commission of enquiry.

It seems to me that the Prime Minister's explanation regarding the lack of jurisdiction in Hong Kong, however true, should not preclude the commission of enquiry in Kuala Lumpur. Whether it is the present committee or a commission of enquiry, the fact remains the same, that it cannot operate effectively outside Malaysia. But it would have been much more effective if a commission of enquiry had set out to do the work which the committee has done, even though it was restricted to Malaysia.

Apart from this, there is another possibility against which the above argument does not hold. A Royal Commission of Enquiry could be set up on the parent body itself, the BBMB. After all, it was the BBMB that allowed the situation to prevail. As Tun Hussein Onn said, the condition in the BBMB was no better than in the BMF. Only the scale of the scandal was exaggerated. There are many scandals involving the BMF all over the country, of which the BMF (Hong Kong) scandal is the climax. The affliction is widespread and affects other areas as well. Professor Ungku Aziz, the Vice-Chancellor of the University of Malaya, for instance, vigorously complained of the abuses in the co-operative movement. Many indulged in lending huge sums of money to their office-bearers. Leaders tended to manipulate the members who did not participate in the decision-making process. Their participation was limited to being taken to meetings in buses to applaud the directors. They were thus treated like goats and turkeys.[30]

Corruption is not only rampant in the developing societies but has developed in scope and degree to the point of becoming a continuing calamity. The greatest damage done to society is the weakening of the will to fight it and the gradual acceptance of corruption as a way of life amongst those in power. The moral aversion against corruption is weak. In such a setting, official pronouncements can play a crucial role. Do they dampen the spirit or invigorate the will? In the case of the BMF scandal, official pronouncements tended to dampen the spirit. One thing is certain, the perpetrators of the crime were happy to hear them.

Time and again it was said that one was innocent until proven guilty, that the culprits could not be tried under Malaysian law, that it took time to obtain evidence, that careful investigation had to be conducted and that the scandal should not be turned into a witch-hunt. While such ideas were public knowledge, the very fact that they were repeatedly emphasized in relation to the BMF scandal had the tendency to dampen the spirit and create anxiety that the public interest was not vigorously safeguarded. We shall not go into detail but suffice to say that the public requires a continuing stream of information of the kind that enhances the morale. Some instances are relevant.

Tan Sri Ahmad Noordin stated that 350 of the 900 government firms have been continuously losing money amounting to millions for years. He was commenting on Finance Minister Daim Zainuddin's call that chief executives and directors of failed government companies and statutory bodies resign voluntarily.[31] The practice of retaining useless directors should be stopped. In Sabah, Deputy Chief Minister Ahmad Baharom Titingan revealed the rampant abuse of funds in local authorities throughout the state, amounting to something possibly staggering.[32]

Some Malaysian political leaders and cabinet ministers have several times voiced their concern regarding corruption and inefficiency. Both within the government and the opposition, the subject of corruption has been given attention but the crucial factor is what the government does. Pronouncements against corruption have been made all along, including many by those who are corrupt. Despite such pronouncements, we know that corruption in the developing societies has continued to grow. This phenomenon requires explanation. Amongst the most decisive causes is the nature of leadership. Earlier, we alluded to the moral quality of leadership as a crucial factor. You cannot expect a corrupt leadership to wipe out corruption. However, there are other factors besides moral quality that could impede the successful effort against corruption. These are weaknesses in the leadership and an inability to perceive problems.

LEADERSHIP AND ROLE OF THE PRESS

There have been instances in history where a leader was personally not corrupt but was surrounded by corrupt supporters. Such a leader is worse than a corrupt one from the point of view of eliminating corruption. His historical function is to act as a shield and deflector. Due to his presence, the semblance of a clean government is projected, thereby deflecting the polluting rays of corruption emanating from the government of which he is head. His presence creates a false sense of security. Sooner or later, he will be succeeded by a corrupt leader. He does not attract public resentment because he is not corrupt while at the same time the corrupt operate freely during the period of his leadership. Such a leader is either weak or opportunistic. Hence the presence of weak leaders who are not corrupt in a thoroughly corrupt set-up by no means mitigates against corruption.

The perception of the problem by the leadership, if it is not accurate, can also act as an impediment to the eradication of corruption. Third World countries seriously affected by corruption are in a position to provide institutional safeguards against it but the will to do so is lacking. Two examples are the introductions of the Ombudsman as in Pakistan and the vigilance committee as in India. The question of their effectiveness does not arise. At least they can keep the effort alive. If we argue on the principle of effectiveness alone, then so many other measures would have to be given up. The eradication of poverty, the attainment of optimum employment, the control of population growth, the raising of the general standard of living have all lacked effectiveness. Yet we do not say 'stop trying'. The same holds for corruption.

Four months before the BMF Committee of Enquiry was formed, I suggested in a dialogue session on 'The Problems of Corruption throughout History', with members of the press in Johore Bahru, on 11 September 1983, that the Anti-Corruption Agency in Malaysia should publish an annual report for the public. By doing so, the public would have more confidence in the agency. Apart from this, it was also suggested that the Malaysian government set up a vigilance committee empowered to investigate and keep tabs on corruption in different government agencies, departments and ministries. Such a committee has been in operation in India for more than a decade. Similarly, the anti-corruption agency in Hong Kong has been publishing its annual report for years.[33]

Measures such as those proposed above should not be taken in isolation of the entire context of the situation. It is like eradicating the plague. Everything about it has to be known and everything against it has to be done. The total approach in the struggle against corruption is the only promising one. Here the press has a vital role in keeping the memory alive and the spirit burning. But a more analytic and investigative spirit is required than the mere publication of news items. Follow-up stories should be written as much as possible.

One instance is fresh in my mind. In April 1986, a dam in Sri Lanka burst, killing at least 100 people, inundating dozens of villages. At least 30,000 people were made homeless when water from the Kantalai reservoir, 230 kilometres from Colombo, rushed through the cracks in the dam. According to radio reports, 10,000 houses were destroyed. The interesting thing is that this disaster revealed the degree of negligence surrounding the security of the dam. Weeks before it happened residents had complained that the dam was in danger of bursting.[34] It would have been much more desirable if such news was followed by further investigative reporting. Certain questions could be raised. Was corruption involved in the construction of the dam? Was the lack of attention a result of low morale brought about by a corrupt and decadent climate? We have stressed the vital and positive role of the press against corruption. For the press to be really effective, we need the freedom of expression and journalists such as Lincoln Steffens, the father of the modern American resistance against corruption, who died in 1936. His books and articles did a great deal to awaken resistance against corruption.[35] However, even in this area, you have the supporters of corrupt regimes or those with a permissive attitude towards corruption. The level of morality in the psyche varies with different journalists as it does with different people. This attitude appears in their writings and at times it can be obstructive.

It is a well-known and accepted fact that the past regime of President Ferdinand Marcos of the Philippines was riddled with corruption at an unprecedented scale. Disclosures of such corruption spread all over the world. At the time when the new popular government of Mrs Corazon Aquino was beginning to grapple with the situation, an editorial review of *The Asian Wall Street Journal* did something which would make the corrupt happy. It started to cast doubts on the efficacy of Mrs Aquino's measures. This was what it said: 'Everyone seems haunted by old ghosts in Manila these days. The hunt for Mr Marcos's "hidden wealth", and Imelda's hidden closets, has become voyeuresque. Report in the Manila papers hint darkly that Mr Marcos is manipulating his former allies with phone calls from Hawaii, perhaps plotting a return. Mrs Aquino has also frozen the assets of suspected Marcos cronies—a blow to the property rights that will be crucial to any economic recovery, *even if some of that wealth was obtained through corruption.*'[36]

The Asian Wall Street Journal is to be credited for its interest in highlighting corruption in its numerous informative articles. But this particular editorial is incongruous with its general trend and criticizing corrupt regimes. Those who had amassed property through corruption would be very pleased with such an editorial. The editorial does not understand that it is corruption that sabotaged the economic recovery of the Philippines during the Marcos era. Freezing the assets of corrupt individuals is one of those measures necessary to recover what is lost through corruption. Instead of getting support for her attempts, Mrs Aquino received what amounted to a ridicule.

ON MAN'S INHUMANITY

The degree of dehumanization effected by corruption in Third World countries is so astounding that any attempt to resist it should get maximum response. The cluster phenomenon of corruption, i.e. its interweaving with other negative elements earlier mentioned such as negligence, lethargy, inefficiency and callous disregard for human suffering, would make exaggerated concern for issues such as property rights a triviality. As we have noted earlier in the book, it is the totality of the phenomenon that we should consider, the totality of its inhuman effects. It is not only human society that becomes its victim, the natural environment is also affected.

A case in point is the unprecedented Indonesian forest fires that occurred during the late 1982 and early 1983. Wildfires devastated 3.5 million hectares of land in East Kalimantan, an area 56 times the size of Singapore and roughly the size of the island of Taiwan. Billions of dollars were lost and the livelihood of thousands was threatened. There were several causes of the fire, direct and indirect, and corruption was one of them. The wildfires originated around drought-stricken areas from small agricultural settlements. Indiscriminate logging with its deadwood residue created attractive paths for wildfires. Enforcement of the selective logging system was inadequate.[37] Corruption played a role in the occurence of the forest fires.

As we have indicated earlier, corruption forms a cluster with other negative elements such as negligence, inefficiency, callousness and lack of human feeling. I would like to end this discussion with some recent examples from Pakistan. In February 1986, three bereaved parents sent an appeal to the President of Pakistan in connection with the disappearance of their three sons, who had been sent by an auditing firm from Lahore to Rawalpindi. They left on 14 November 1985, and on 2 December 1985, the parents learned that their boys were supposed to have travelled in a bus that plunged into the River Indus on 1 December 1985. The bus was retrieved on 14 December, but the bodies of the bus driver and the three boys were not found. Those of twenty-six other passengers were found.

The parents wrote twenty-seven letters to the President, seven to the Prime Minister, six to the Governor of the Punjab, four to the Chief Minister of the Punjab, three each to the Ministers of Justice and Parliamentary Affairs, Minister for Northern Areas and the Speaker of the National Assembly, two each to the Commander-in-Chief, Pakistan Army, and the previous Railways Minister. All these fifty-six letters were not even acknowledged except the one to the Speaker of the National Assembly.[38] Such absence of sympathy and compassion on the part of the authority was glaring. In a corrupt-ridden society, sympathy and compassion are not powerful considerations.

Another instance, this time directly connected with corruption, was the suicide of an elderly couple in Lahore, an 85-year-old man and his 70-year-old wife, on the night of 30 July 1986. Apparently they committed suicide after suffering four days of police treatment. They were asked to raise Rs 7,000 for the release of their son from custody, or have their daughters locked up at the police station. Later, thousands demonstrated in sympathy for the elderly couple.[39]

Prime Minister Mohammad Khan Junejo took a serious view of the harassment and illegal detention of relatives of political workers wanted by the police. During a press conference at the Lahore airport on 24 August 1906, he was informed that the police did not allow a political worker to attend the funeral of his infant son in Lahore recently.[40]

There was also the case of an innocent man hanged to death for a murder he did not commit. Before dying, the victim who had been attacked at dusk, visualized in his mind the assailant. The man, with twelve others, was arrested. In the process, the investigating officer summoned every able-bodied man in the village and extorted money from them. The accused was hanged. The lawyer engaged in the defence of some of the accused was visited by an old client one evening while the preliminary enquiry was going on, together with a young man. 'He disclosed that the young fellow had actually killed the man with his spear but the deceased was obsessed with "X" whom he had named as the assailant.'[41]

The founder of Pakistan, Mohammad Ali Jinnah, in his first presidential address to Pakistan's Constituent Assembly on 12 August 1947, stressed that one of the biggest problems from which the country was suffering was bribery and corruption which must be put down with an iron hand.[42] Throughout history, voices have been raised against corruption. The great Muslim theologian and philosopher Abu Hamid al-Ghazzali (AD 1058–1111), dwelled upon corruption in several of his letters to several prime ministers of his state, under the Selyuq dynasty. In one addressed to Mujiruddin, he said: 'As soon as possible and so far as it lies within your power, you should spare no pains to ensure that corruption, nepotism, injustice, bribery, cruelty and other ills are completely wiped out. The people are the glory of our kingdom and the source of its wealth. You do not know the present state of their finance. You can have no idea of an anarchy that exists in this part of the country. The corrupt revenue officials exploit the ignorant masses for their own profit and do not credit the amount of taxes and other government dues (charged at exorbitant rates) into the government treasury. Think upon your subjects, broken in body and groaning under poverty and hunger. Their limbs tremble under them. Long anxiety has reduced them to a skeleton, while you are leading a life of luxury and indifference.'[43]

More resounding was the warning of Sari Mehmed Pasha, a Treasurer of the Ottoman Empire, who was executed in 1717 as a victim of intrigue. He said: 'Bribery is the beginning and root of all illegality and tyranny, the source and fountain of every sort of disturbance and sedition, the most vast of evils and greatest of calamities. It is the mine of corruption than which there is nothing whatever more calamitous to the people of Islam or more destructive to the foundations of religion and government. Than this there is no more powerful engine of injustice and cruelty, for bribery destroys both faith and state.[44]

There is no lack of judgement against corruption in the past. The ravages of corruption have been known all along. The historical settings differ but the serious effects remain, expressing themselves in various manifestations. The cluster effect is the most serious and persistent. Not only is there immediate damage, but the accompanying phenomena of negligence, inefficiency, indolence and low morale, interwoven with the process of corruption, have persisted throughout the ages. To break this trend is the task of the present and succeeding generations of those concerned with the well-being future of human society. As to the corrupt, they care not for any lofty ideal.

Endnotes

1. *The Pakistan Times Overseas Weekly* (*TPTOW*), Lahore, 22 December 1985.

2. *TPTOW*, 'Rooting Out Corruption', Lahore, 12 January 1986, p. 2.

3. *Ibid.* The *Wafaqi Mohtasib* is the Pakistani term for Ombudsman.

4. *TPTOW*, 'Cancer of Corruption', Lahore, 29 September 1985, p. 2.

5. *Ibid.*

6. *Ibid.*

7. *TPTOW*, 'Roots of Corruption', Lahore, 2 March 1986, p. 2.

8. *Ibid.*

9. *TPTOW*, Lahore, 7 April 1985, p. 15.

10. *Ibid.*

11. Mohammad Idrees, 'Let's Extend *Mohtasib's* Jurisdiction', *TPTOW*, Lahore, 24 June 1984, p. 4.

12. Quoted in Mohammad Idrees, 'Let All Patriots Help the *Mohtasib*', *TPTOW*, 17 June 1984, p. 4.

13. *TPTOW*, Lahore, 10 June 1984, p. 5.

14. *Kompas*, Jakarta, 29 September 1983. See also that of 28 September 1983.

15. *The Star*, Kuala Lumpur, 17 October 1983.

16. On the entire affair, see Appendix A.

17. BMF *Committee of Enquiry Final Report*, vol. 2, p. 938.

18. *Ibid.*

19. *Ibid.*, p. 939.

20. *Special Brief*, BBMB, Kuala Lumpur, 1986, p. 242.

21. *Special Brief*, BBMB, Kuala Lumpur, 1986, Part 2, p. 373.

22. *Special Brief*, Part 3, p. 332.

23. BMF *Committee of Enquiry Final Report*, vol. 1, pp. 421–5.

24. *The Straits Times*, Singapore, 17 May 1986.

25. *Op. cit.*, *Lampiran IV* (a).

26. *Ibid.*, *Lampiran IV* (a), (b) and *Lampiran V* (a).

27. Syed Hussein Alatas, '*Ke Arah Integrasi Nasional*', *Kertas Kerja* (Working Paper), *Khemah Kerja Politik Barisan Nasional*, Morib, Selangor, 1–3 February 1986.

28. *The New Straits Times*, Kuala Lumpur, 8 January 1985. Tun Hussein Onn came to know of the scandal through the press. See this issue.

29. *Malaysian Digest*, Kuala Lumpur, vol. 15, no. 1, 15 January 1984. On Mr Lim's views, see his 'The BMF Scandal', Kuala Lumpur, 1983. Speech in Parliament, 24 October 1983.

30. *The Star*, Kuala Lumpur, 17 June 1986. See p. 11, the report on his speech at a co-operative seminar.

31. *The Star*, Kuala Lumpur, 27 June 1986.

32. *The New Straits Times*, Kuala Lumpur, 28 June 1986.

33. *The New Straits Times*, 12 September 1983; *The Star*, 12 September 1983; *Utusan Malaysia*, 12 September 1983. See also Appendix B.

34. *The Straits Times*, Singapore, 22 April 1986.

35. On his life, see Justin Kaplan, *Lincoln Steffens*, Jonathan Cape, London, 1975.

36. *The Asian Wall Street Journal*, 31 March 1986. Italics are mine.

37. On this, see 'Wound in the World', *Asia Week*, Hong Kong, 13 July 1984.

38. Mohd. Idrees, 'The Case of the Missing Auditors', *TPTOW*, 3 August 1986, p. 4.

39. Mohd. Idrees, 'The System that Failed the Suicide Couple', *TPTOW*, 10 August 1986, p. 12.

40. *TPTOW*, 31 August 1986.

41. *Ibid.* See Editor's Mail, p. 2.

42. *Ibid.*

43. Abdul Qayyum, *Letters of Al-Ghazzali*, Islamic Publications, Lahore, 1976, p. 97.

44. Sari Mehmed Pasha, *Ottoman Statecraft*, tr. W. L. Wright, Princeton University Press, Princeton, 1936, p. 88.

Chapter 4

CORRUPTION AND THE IDEALS OF EXCELLENCE

THE present Singapore society is a fertile source for reflecting on the problem of corruption. We mean by the problem of corruption not the mere existence of corruption, here and there. This is present in Singapore. Crime is present everywhere but it is not the same as the control of authority by criminal elements. When we say there is no problem of corruption in Singapore we mean that the authority is not dominated and manipulated by corrupt elements; that it is possible for a generation to go through life without having to bribe government servants in their transactions with the authority; that taxes are properly collected; that the courts are not at the service of the corrupt; that the police perform their duty without bribes; and so do other services for the public.

The question to raise is how has Singapore managed to be what it is? To answer this question let us follow the discussion carried out by Karl Marx against Victor Hugo. Hugo's error, according to Karl Marx, consists in ascribing historical events, in this case those around Louis Bonaparte, to the conduct of an individual (Louis Bonaparte): 'Reasoning from general principles—the general principles of society, laid down by the ruling classes and embodied in their very creeds, Victor Hugo judges from an erroneous point of view; he sees in the man the motive power, instead of seeking for it in class interests, class antagonism, and class revolution, while the man is the mere temporary exponent of the change—as the weathercock betokens the direction of the wind. Victor Hugo belongs to a class who thus look on the effect as the cause—on the instrument as the hand that uses it.'[1]

Marx objects to the habit of attributing lofty moral ideals to the pure and genuine motivation of the middle class propounding them. He says, 'In that class, certainly there are those who denounce the inequalities and horrors of the present system with a violence and a declamatory force often superior to the expressions of the very revolutionary class itself. To hear them one would believe that they are more socialist than the whole of the working class. And what are they in fact? They are reactionary. I shall not call them knaves; perhaps they are unconscious of the real tendency of their doctrines and actions, although in our present age illusions are hardly possible to men, who live in contact with the actual world. But most certainly are they the dupes of the class notions, instilled into their minds as the general principles of social life.'[2]

The middle class does not question the principles of social life but instead blames individuals for not living up to the principles. It is in this connection that he attacks Victor Hugo. 'In his [Hugo's] eyes the principles of present social government are right, and the men to be blamed. That is the opinion of all moralising middle-class reformers. Whatever there is wrong and perverted, pernicious and deleterious, it is the fault of the individuals—and the classes who support those individuals? Oh, they never think of classes. Far from them the misanthropical conception of a society composed of classes and ruled by class-interest.'[3]

Such middle-class morality attempts to reform the individuals. The rest follows. The government would then be perfect. Marx further comments: 'They always treat the people as a whole, address it as a whole, suppose them of the same creed, with one common conscience, with one universal opinion. Take that for granted, and those men would seem the greatest (would-be) benefactors of humanity, the initiators of a new era, the restorers of the paradise lost. Drive them from this ground, show the people that there is neither a community of morals, nor of conscience, nor of opinion ever possible between different classes with opposed interests, that the institutions of a class produce not only with necessity those facts over which our philanthropists lament, but also the men, whom they accuse of all the mischievous arrangements in the body politic—and from the dignity of demi-gods you reduce them to the nullity of sham-prophets.'[4]

Marx is arguing against those who view morality in isolation from the class interest prompting its formulation. Here we have a relevant example of his treatment of corruption. The emergence of the anti-corruption trend in the British election he discusses is due to the interest of the bourgeoisie. Writing in 1852, he notes that British elections had traditionally been corrupt until the relative positions of classes and parties underwent a radical change from the moment the industrial and commercial middle classes took up a stand as an official party at the side of the Whigs and Tories.

This bourgeoisie was not fond of expensive election campaigns: 'They considered it cheaper to compete with the landed aristocracy by general moral, than by personal pecuniary means. On the other hand they were conscious of representing a universally predominant interest of modern society. They were, therefore, in a position to demand that electors should be ruled by their common national interests, not by personal and local motives, and the more they recurred to this postulate, the more the latter species of electoral influence was, by the very composition of constituencies, centered in the landed aristocracy, but withheld from the middle classes. Thus the Bourgeoisie contended for the principle of moral elections and forced the enactment of laws in that sense, intended, each of them, as safeguards against the local influence of the landed aristocracy; and indeed, from 1831 down, bribery adopted a more civilized, more hidden form, and general elections went off in a more sober way than before.'[5]

THE CLASS-INTEREST FACTOR AND THE HISTORICAL CONTEXT

Consequently, the increase of corruption as well as its decrease is due to the class-interest factor operating in a historical context. The role of the individual antagonists of corruption is conditioned by the historical context. Marx does not pay much attention to the role of the individual in the historical process. This is where a need is felt for the extension of the historical method. We shall try to focus attention on this factor by drawing our instances from the Singapore experience. But before that let us briefly enumerate the causes of corruption in contemporary Asia following World War II. The war and the independence of Asian countries from Western rule figure prominently in the outburst of corruption characterizing the post-war period. Under colonial rule there was corruption but its dynamics and phenomenology took a drastic turn following the independence of the country. This drastic turn was mainly due to: (1) widespread corruption during the war period preceding the achievement of independence; (2) the sudden increase in administration; (3) the sudden increase in opportunities for corruption at a bigger and higher scale; (4) the invasion of the different levels of leadership by people of low moral integrity; (5) the inexperience of leaders fighting for independence in building a clean and efficient government; and (6) the manipulation and intrigues of foreign financial and business powers through means of corruption.

The case of India is instructive from the above point of view. In 1962 several Members of Parliament (MPs) referred to the growing menace of corruption in the administration. A committee was formed by the then Minister of Home Affairs, Lal Bahadur Shastri, headed by an MP, K. Santhanam. The final report of the committee, called the Santhanam Report, was handed to the government on 31 March 1964. What concerns us here is the analysis of the causes of corruption and the measures suggested to prevent it. We shall select those parts relevant to our purpose. Henceforth this document will be referred to as the Report. For emphasis, sections of the report which have been mentioned earlier, are repeated.

First, there is the difference between the past and present bureaucracies: 'In the primitive and medieval societies the scope of public authority was small; many of the matters that were looked after by the community have now become a function of the State. The few authorities which existed for the collection of taxes, administration of justice or other purposes did not act according to any definite written laws or rules, but largely at their discretion subject to good conscience and equity and directives from the higher authorities. So long as the officials were loyal to the existing regime and did not resort to oppression and forcible expropriation, they were free to do as they liked.'[6]

Next, the corruptive influence of World War II: 'The immense war efforts during 1939 to 1945 which involved an annual expenditure of hundreds of crores of rupees over all kinds of war supplies and contracts created unprecedented opportunities for acquisition of wealth by doubtful means. The wartime controls and scarcities provided ample opportunities for bribery, corruption, favouritism, etc. The then Government subordinated all other considerations to that of making the war effort a success. Propriety of means was no consideration if it impeded the war effort. It would not be far wrong to say that the high water mark of corruption was reached in India as perhaps in other countries also, during the period of the Second World War.'[7]

Before the war, according to the Report, corruption was prevalent among low-level officials. The higher ranks were comparatively free of it. Lack of fluid resources set limits to the opportunities and capacity for corruption. After the transfer of power at the time of independence, there were patriotism and high ideals. Attempts were made to check the spread of corruption, but they were thwarted: '... various factors have operated to nullify in some measure the anti-corruption drive. The sudden extension of the economic activities of the Government with a large armoury of regulations, controls, licences and permits provided new and large opportunities. The quest for political power at different levels made successful achievement of the objective more important than the means adopted. Complaints against the highly placed in public life were not dealt with in the manner that they should have been dealt with if public confidence had to be maintained. Weakness in this respect created cynicism and the growth of the belief that while Governments were against corruption they were not against corrupt individuals, if such individuals had the requisite amount of power, influence, and protection.'[8]

At the same time rapid urbanization brought about the weakening of rural values. Social controls resulting in the maintenance of frugality and simplicity of life were replaced by those encouraging materialism, impersonalism, status craving, greed for money and power, and an unwillingness to adhere to moral values. In this climate the business and commercial classes, whose ranks were swelled by speculators and adventurers of the war period, exerted their corruptive influence. The salaried classes meanwhile experienced a decline in real income. The larger part of these classes belonged to government service. All these formed a fertile soil for corruption.

There were also the cumbersome and dilatory procedures and practices in the working of government offices. This gave rise to the 'speed money' type of corruption. 'Generally the bribe giver does not wish, in these cases, to get anything done unlawfully, but wants to speed up the process of the movement of files and communications relating to decisions. Certain sections of the staff concerned are reported to have got into the habit of not doing anything in the matter till they are suitably persuaded.'[9]

The scope and incentives for corruption were greatest at the points where important decisions that would substantially affect the fortunes of interested groups or individuals were taken: such as in the assessment and collection of taxes, obtaining licences and contracts, or in orders for supplies. It was suggested that the corruption cost was between 7 and 11 per cent in undertakings done for the government.[10] The Report finally took into account businessmen and industrialists as the greatest corrupting influences on a major and organized scale. 'To these, corruption is not only an easy method to secure large unearned profits but also the necessary means to enable them to be in a position to pursue their vocations or retain their position among their own competitors. It is to these persons who indulge in evasion and avoidance of taxes, accumulate large amounts of unaccounted money by various methods such as obtaining licences in the names of bogus firms and individuals, trafficking in licences, suppressing profits by manipulation of accounts to avoid taxes and other legitimate claims on profits, accepting money for transactions put through without accounting for it in bills and accounts (on-money) and under-valuation of transactions in immovable property. It is they who have control over large funds and are in a position to spend considerable sums of money in entertainment. It is they who maintain an army of liaison men and contact men, some of whom live, spend and entertain ostentatiously. We are unable to believe that so much money is being spent only for the purpose of getting things done quickly.'[11]

The Report further mentioned the activity of these contact men in subverting the integrity of government servants. 'The tendency to subvert integrity in the public services instead of being isolated and aberrative is growing into an organized, well-planned racket.'[12] In addition to such attempts, there was the offer of employment to retired government servants by the commercial and industrial sector. 'It is generally believed that such employment is secured in many cases as a *quid pro quo* for favours shown by the Government servant while in service. It is also feared that high placed Government servants who accept such employment after retirement may be in a position, by virtue of their past standing, to exercise undue influence on Government servants in service who might have been their colleagues or subordinates. The fact that some of these retired Government servants who have accepted employment with private firms live in Delhi and perhaps operate as "contact men" has further heightened these supicions.'[13]

Before we go further, let us enquire what is meant by the general historical condition. The present Southeast Asia is under the same general historical condition. The economic system of its ASEAN countries is capitalism. The degree and manifestation of corruption in Thailand, the Philippines, Indonesia, Malaysia and Singapore differs greatly. In Thailand, the Philippines and Indonesia, corruption is rampant. In Malaysia it is not rampant, and in Singapore it is hardly noticeable. The differential development of corruption in these countries cannot be explained by the capitalist system. Furthermore, capitalism in Western European countries is not associated with corrupt governments. Consequently, here capitalism by itself cannot be the cause of widespread corruption.

This type of widespread corruption I have called tidal corruption. It is one that floods the entire state apparatus including the centre of power, immersing everything in its path. It multiplies the number of perpetrators more rapidly than any other type of criminal behaviour, paralysing the administrative machinery and dampening the enthusiasm of sincere and capable civil servants.[14] That tidal corruption is not confined to any particular social and economic order is now obvious. Certain communist countries of the Third World have the same problem. Russia itself is grappling with a serious problem of corruption. Marx's explanation of corruption in England does not apply to Russia and China.

The inadequacy of the historical–context approach as presented by Marxists and certain functional sociologists is apparent from their failure to explain both corruption as a universal phenomenon affecting all complex social systems in all ages and its different manifestations within the same system at different times. The Marxists analysis does not descend to a level sufficiently microscopic to see the operation of hitherto neglected organisms. It is at this level of analysis that we find the significant causes of corruption, the most immediate and decisive, the leadership and their cliques.

THE HISTORICAL IDEALS OF EXCELLENCE

Every leadership is influenced by what Huizinga, the well-known Dutch historian, calls 'historical ideals of life'. A historical life-ideal may be defined as any concept of excellence man projects into the past. Some are general, inspiring a whole cultural period; some are valid for a state or a nation; and some accompany a single person's life.[15] What concerns us here is the life-ideal of the single person. The example cited by Huizinga is Charles the Bold (1433–77), the last Duke of Burgundy, whose ideals to emulate were the commanders of antiquity. Charles XII of Sweden (1682–1718) had Gustavus Adolphus (1594–1692) in mind in his struggle for power. His life was a conscious imitation of Gustavus Adolphus's life. He even hoped to die in the same way as his hero.[16]

As Huizinga pointed out, the historical ideal suggests a certain line of development over long periods. 'In early periods of civilization they are mythical, lacking a true historical basis. They are ideals of pure happiness, very vaguely conceived and very distant. Gradually the recollection of an actual past comes to play a larger role—the historical content increases, and the ideals become more specific and closer at hand. While the ideal of perfect happiness is gazed after disconsolately, lost for ever, the need arises to live in keeping with the ideal. Not only the historical quality has increased but also the ethical.'[17]

The historical ideal of excellence with a high ethical content embodied in great personalities of the past conditions to a great extent how the leaders moved by its spirit react to corruption and injustice (owing to the factor of emulation noted earlier). Likewise if the historical ideal lacks ethical content, it will influence those under its spell in the same direction. There were cases in history where a ruler abdicated because he could not conform to the historical ideal of his group. Mu'awiyah II, the grandson of the founder of the Umayyah dynasty, abdicated the throne after a reign of a few months in AD 683. It is said that he abhorred the crimes of his family. He was not able to live up to what they considered to be the right kind of ruler. He confessed he did not possess enough strength to do indecent things to live up to the tradition of his dynastic ancestors.[18]

The historical ideal asserts itself vigorously during a critical situation. An interesting instance is Ibn al-Sikkit, one of the great scholars and figures in Arabic literature. He was the tutor of the two sons of al-Mutawakkil, the notorious 'Abbasid Caliph who was assassinated by his Turkish guards in AD 861. Mutawakkil asked Ibn al-Sikkit whether his [Mutawakkil's] two sons were dearer to him than Hasan and Husayn, the two sons of 'Ali and grandsons of the Prophet of Islam. Disturbed by the question and becoming very agitated, Ibn al-Sikkit replied that the slave of 'Ali was definitely dearer to him than the two sons of Ibn Mutawakkil plus the father himself.[19] On hearing this, Mutawakkil ordered that Ibn al-Sikkit's tongue be plucked out and that his Turkish guards tread on his belly. He was carried back home and died two days later in AD 858.[20]

The historical ideal of powerful personalities exerts a great influence in history. One of these personalities, 'Ali ibn Abi Talib, the Fourth Righteous Caliph of Islam, was aware of this when he was fighting against the rebellious Mu'awiyah, founder of the Umayyah dynasty. He said that Mu'awiyah (d. AD 680) was not more cunning than he was but allowed himself to apply deceit. 'Ali, assassinated by a member of a fanatical sect in AD 661, remarked that had he not hated deceit, he would have been the most cunning of all men.[21] We need not go into details of historical events manifesting deceit and the reaction of the other party towards it: suffice it to say the influence was great and flowed out of the historical ideal of those in power, and this cannot be explained by general economic conditions unless we confine ourselves to the platitude that people fight to protect their interests.

We shall now discuss the interplay between the historical ideals of those in power and the general socio-economic conditions. For our purpose we shall confine our discussion to the negative and positive historical ideals and how such ideals operate autonomously from general socio-economic conditions and class relations. Let us go back to Singapore. If we adopt the Marxian thesis on resistance against corruption, we could say that corruption endangers the survival of the present group in power. Not only this, but the security of the state can be jeopardized.

If corruption were to spread in the body politic it could easily undermine the position of the leadership. Hostile elements with powerful financial resources abroad could play havoc with their bought-over political figures. One multinational could buy over the entire Cabinet. Owing to its size and geographical location, it would be easy to destroy a government in Singapore through corruption. It follows that the serious stand against corruption taken by the present leadership need not be attributed to a historical ideal but more to circumstances. This is in accord with the Marxian thesis, for it rules out the role of historical ideals and individual personalities as autonomous centres in the field of causation.

Even after we have accepted the influence of general conditions, there is yet the decisive influence of the historical ideal. It is, of course, difficult to identify the ideal because it is generally not revealed in public. The former Prime Minister of Singapore, Mr Lee Kuan Yew, has not discussed in public which great historical personalities he admires; which period of the past attracts him; which revolution enamours him; which sages of the past he respects most. What are the kinds of leaders he looks up to and looks down upon? On which ideal is he moulding himself? What is his idea of social shame and honour?

The above constituents of the historical ideal operate within the general system of causations somewhat autonomously. They can exert a strong influence on society's development. Within the capitalist structure which emphasizes profit and productivity, they condition the kind of profit-making and productivity that takes place. There are profit-making and productive activities which are negative as well as positive. The direction of overall development depends on the kind of dominant leadership that a society has. A convenient and clear illustration is the recent case of a Singapore minister's suicide arising from an investigation of corruption.[22] In many other Asian countries a Cabinet minister of such reputation would have escaped investigation. The Prime Minister considered him to be a man of considerable ability; he clearly was appreciative of his capacity as a Cabinet minister. But the ideal prevails. The Prime Minister said, 'There is no way a Minister can avoid investigations and a trail if there is evidence to support one.'[23] His further remarks on corruption indicate the role of the historical ideal. The image of the ideal government is one dominated by a sense of shame.

The significance of the historical ideal is manifested by the role of the Prime Minister in the context of events and circumstances. According to Mr Lee Kuan Yew, the effectiveness of the system to check or punish corruption rests, first, on the law against corruption; secondly, on a vigilant public to provide information on suspected corruption; and thirdly, on an anti-corruption organization which is scrupulous, thorough, and fearless in its investigations.[24] For this organization to function it has to have the full backing of the Prime Minister under whose portfolio it comes, says Mr Lee. However, Mr Lee cites another factor: 'The strongest deterrent is a public opinion which censures and condemns corrupt persons, in other words, in attitudes which make corruption so unacceptable that the stigma of corruption cannot be washed away by serving a prison sentence.'[25]

What Mr Lee is referring to is the sense of shame.[26] It is this sense of shame and its opposite, the sense of pride, which are sadly lacking amongst the ruling classes of Asia. Mr S. Rajaratnam, then the Minister of Foreign Affairs of Singapore (1968), recounted the effects of corruption arising from the weakness of the historical ideal and the lack of the sense of shame in Asian societies. During the previous two decades, it had become a serious impediment to economic growth and development. It created increasing political instability, dangerous tensions and conflicts in Asia.[27]

What is meant here by the sense of shame is not shame associated with private and individual relations but a shame associated with the collectivity, with the conditions of one's fellow men. It is directed at elements threatening human welfare and dignity. 'It is undignified to have a dirty surrounding. It is undignified to live in a disorderly and haphazard manner. It is undignified to be subjected to petty corruption and rude treatment. It is undignified to be cheated of your rights. It is undignified to be governed by men with criminal minds, men who spend most of their time plotting to cheat and plunder the state.'[28]

The above is best explained by an illustration. The corrupt person is devoid of this particular sense of shame. 'A bureaucrat goes to the market and stops in front of a fruit stall. The stall-keeper isn't there. He waits for him to return and buys his fruit. He doesn't steal any of the fruit. He would feel ashamed to do so. It would violate his self-respect. His inner conscience rejects such behaviour. In the office things are different. This same bureaucrat steals government money on a considerable scale. His serious thinking time in the office is spent plotting and covering his large-scale corruption. He has no sense of shame as far as public interest is concerned.'[29]

In the personality of such a person is found a split morality which is often transmitted to his children. When this has gone on for some time the entire society experiences a lowered level of shame. S. Rajaratnam describes the effect: 'In what is essentially an honest society there can be and will be scandalous instances of corruption as there will also be outbreaks of crime and violence. But such a society will make every effort to restrain, detect and punish those who attempt to deviate from the standards of honesty that it upholds and respects. It will not honour and encourage into positions of power and prestige the corrupt men who have successfully circumvented the law.'[30]

As far as Singapore and countries in similar conditions are concerned, the historical ideal moulding the self-image of those in power is a much more important defence against corruption than the general economic conditions exerting their influence on the leadership. The historical ideal conditions the self-image and motivations of the leaders. How would they want to be remembered in history? Corrupt leaders have corrupt historical ideals. In their personalities there is no inner drive to emulate the great men of history or to live up to a certain ideal requiring struggle and tension.

A recent instance is available from Russia. In his report as General Secretary of the Communist Party of the Soviet Union to its Central Committee, at its plenary meeting on 27 January 1987, Mikhail Gorbachov attempted what amounts to a revival of the historical ideal in the face of stagnation, decadence and corruption affecting the body politic. He said: 'Elements of social corrosion that emerged in the past few years had a negative effect on society's morale and inconspicuously eroded the lofty moral values which have always been characteristic of our people and of which we are proud, namely, ideological dedication, labour enthusiasm and Soviet patriotism.'[31]

This is perhaps the most candid and earnest report delivered by a state leader on the conditions and problems of his society. Practically all the major problems are mentioned. One is the degeneration of party cadres. Among them were those guilty of embezzlement, bribe-taking, report-padding, and heavy drinking. Some even became accomplices in, if not organizers of, criminal activities. The entire society is affected by a cluster of problems. 'Loose discipline and a lowering of responsibility are too deeply rooted and are felt painfully to this day. It is precisely criminal irresponsibility and carelessness, which are the main causes of such tragic events as the accident at the Chernobyl nuclear power plant, the sinking of the *Admiral Nakhimov*, a number of air and railway accidents, which involved human casualties.'[32]

In this attempt to direct and reinforce a new moral atmosphere shaping the country, Gorbachov more than once referred to Lenin as his example. 'This is not just a tribute of great respect, not only an acknowledgement of Lenin's authority. This reflects the pressing desire to revive in modern conditions and revive to the fullest extent possible the spirit of Leninism, to assert in our life the Leninist demands on cadres. You will recall, Comrades, how passionately, how tirelessly Lenin taught that the success of revolutionary struggle, the success of any cardinal restructuring of society is determined in many ways by the mood set by the Party.'[33]

The operation and function of the historical ideal are clearly reflected in Gorbachov's thought. They are particularly operative when society is confronted with problems of morality. The historical ideal embodied in certain leading personalities of the past engenders a more profound consciousness of the moral problem, so that it is recognized as the condition of solving various other problems. As Gorbachov said, 'Lastly, the most important demand is the high moral standard of our cadres, such human qualities as honesty, incorruptibility and modesty. We now know not only from the past but also from recent experience that we would not be able to resolve the tasks involved in reorganization without strengthening society's moral health. It is not coincidental that we have so painfully encountered negative phenomena today in the moral and ethical sphere. I mean that effort to eradicate drunkenness, embezzlement, bribery, abuse of office and protectionism.'[34]

The phenomena of decadence, corruption, low morale and indiscipline recounted by Gorbachov cannot be explained by Marxism without recourse to the autonomous influence of the historical ideal. The rise and decline of such an ideal is not to be explained by general economic conditions which for some decades have remained relatively unchanged in Russia, but by the kind of leadership that has emerged in Russian society. The interplay between different power groups in the Communist Party, in the power hierarchy, conditioned the type of leaders that emerged. Society can suffer under corruption for decades without a leader emerging to struggle against it. When he does emerge, it is not the mere existence of widespread corruption that conditions it. It is the historical ideal of a successful contending group that is decisive.

It may be suggested that nothing in history is autonomous. By autonomous we do not mean absence of causes and conditions. By autonomous we mean that it is not a derivative phenomenon, a reflection of another set of conditions alien to itself. There are in Soviet Russia today leaders whose negative historical ideal is contrary to that of Gorbachov, who accept the situation, who are unwilling to reform, who are used to the decadent climate, who are not eager to emulate Lenin, who pay lip service to the ideals of communism. Theoretically the presence of a variety of human types within a given social and historical setting cannot be entirely explained by external structural and situational causes. The human type reacting within this context to a great extent conditions itself.

Marxism has paid a lot of attention to conflicts between classes, between ideologies, but it has not dealt with conflict between human types within the same class and location in the social and political hierarchy. Stalin, Kruschev, Brezhnev and Gorbachov do not all belong to the same type. Who comes to power is crucial to the development of society. In the process of winning power, as well as the actual exercise of power, the historical ideal has its own autonomous influence. If the successful contender is not infused by a sound historical ideal, then consequences will flow from this. He will surround himself with men of his kind just as his opposite counterpart will.

In contemporary social science hardly any attention is given to the theme of the historical ideal. It is considered as belonging to the realms of religion and philosophy yet its effects and functions, as well as its dynamic, should be the concern of the social sciences. The attitude of leaders towards corruption depends on their historical ideal. Whom do they respect as their example? What kind of society do they wish to have? Whither do they look in the past? What is their sense of pride and shame? What is their conception of service? What memory would they leave behind? What loyalty do they attract? All these revolve around the theme of the historical ideal.

Education, career success, wealth and power are no guarantee against corruption. When the leadership of society has a low level of morality, it will allow disruptive forces to operate and undermine social morality. This statement has to be elucidated by an illustration. Take education and the emphasis on meritocracy. This has to be saddled with a strong sense of morality to restrain the negative effects of the competition on which meritocracy is based. Competition can be corrosive of morality. The violations of morality taking place in the intensity of competition often are not criminal in nature but may conduce to it in the sense that human sentiments clustering around a particular moral value may be eroded, thereby making it easier for corruption to take place.

Take a student who hides books from the library shelves so that others may not read them. Already this behaviour corrodes sentiments of concern and goodwill for others. It emanates from the egoistic desire to compete using unsportsman-like means. When such an attitude prevails widely it can easily slip over into corruption. The corrosion of morality in various areas has always been the antecedent of corruption. Thus we see the serious corruption in many contemporary Asian societies as continuous with antecedent violations of moral values from other areas, such as the degradation of the individual human being in many traditional societies; the absence of the rule of law; continuous exposure to arbitrary rule; immoral myths and folk-tales; an immoral conception of the hero; and many other such manifestations.

It is not my intention here to simplify the social and historical process of development. Whatever is the condition of society; whatever are the problems it faces, in whatever time and place, the historical ideal of those wielding decisive power exerts a great influence. This ideal may not be articulated, or only vaguely conceived, but it is there. It is our thesis here that a weak commitment to the historical ideal amongst the leaders encourages the growth of corruption even if they are not themselves corrupt.

It is obvious that possessing the historical ideal alone is not a sufficient condition for success. How rival groups react, the strength of one's own group, the existence of a strong mass consciousness against corruption: these are some of the factors that should be considered in assessing the prospect of a successful policy against corruption under a leadership influenced by the appropriate historical ideal.[35]

The role and function of the historical ideal should not be taken for granted. It is particularly significant for the top leader wielding enormous power. If the moral constituent of the historical ideal is weak, the consequences can be devastating. This is clear from the behaviour of tyrants and despots. All stratagems have been employed by them, particularly religion owing to its enormous influence amongst the masses. What could be more glaring than the behaviour of al-Mansur, the builder of the 'Abbasid dynasty, who was Caliph for twenty-two years and died in AD 775. His character is said to have been a strange mixture of good and evil. He was very attentive to the public weal but at the same time very cold-blooded, calculating and unscrupulous.[36]

The nature of the man in power conditions the type of the historical ideal he adopts, and this in turn conditions the manner in which he wields his power. Thus in any period of history, independent of the social and economic background, there is this contest of human types manifesting opposing historical ideals. The social and economic background, far from being the cause, can be the effect of this contest. The motivation of those involved is not to be reduced to mere class interest. It goes deeper than this. It springs from the human spirit, which is not a creation of the socio-economic structure.

The human type that wants power, glory and wealth at any cost and by whatever means, the type that is not concerned with the general welfare but only with its own, the type that looks upon lofty moral ideals with cynicism, will eventually clash with its opposite type. This clash is due to the autonomous influence of the historical ideal rather than to the general economic conditions, although these conditions no doubt exert their influence on the development and outcome of the conflict.

The differential reaction of these two human types becomes conspicuous when circumstances have fully unfolded to allow a complete expression of themselves, i.e. their compelling motivation. Islamic history furnishes an interesting instance. Right from the beginning the men around Muhammad were represented by both types. Murtada Mutahhari observes the following: 'In fact, a considerable number of the Prophet's companions were corrupted either by worldly positions and a longing for the Caliphate or by avidity towards money and wealth. This above mentioned principle, however, was not (and is not) a general one; otherwise, all of the Holy Prophet's companions would, God forbid, have trodden the same path and would have been likewise influenced by money and position. Contrary to this, we are familiar with distinguished figures among the companions, who stood firmly against such floods.'[37]

It was very clear that the companions of Muhammad who were averse to corruption such as Abu Bakr, 'Umar and 'Ali, and those around 'Ali, were people influenced by their historical ideal. An excellent example was Abu Dharr Ghifari (d. AD 653) who persistently agitated against corruption in Madinah and Syria during 'Uthman's time until he was exiled to a desert locality with a prohibition against others contacting him. Since he could not be silenced, the only measure left was to isolate him in solitary exile. He and his wife and children, except one daughter, died in the place of exile under severe conditions lacking food and the amenities of life.[38]

Mutahhari, the Iranian scholar and theologian, poses the question: What made Talhah and Zubayr corrupt and Salman and Abu Dharr honest? His answer is that man can have a definite and unchangeable attitude and logic under widely different circumstances. The corrupt do not have this. It is this unchanging moral attitude that is the part of the character of a person that defies reduction to extraneous economic and other forces. The social, economic and historical background of seventh-century Arabia and the surrounding region was the stage on which the drama of 'Ali and Mu'awiyah was enacted, but the nature of the actors was not created by the stage.

Engels attempted to present the Marxist theory of historical development in a manner that would prevent misunderstanding and simplification of the theory. Such a simplification is evident in Mutahhari's treatment of Marxism. Mutahhari understood Marxism as suggesting that an individual changes his mode of thinking according to whether he is rich or poor. The behaviour of Salman Farsi, a close disciple of the Prophet and 'Ali, is presented as an argument against a Marxist interpretation. When Salman became the Governor of Mada'in, his furniture did not exceed a single knapsack which he could carry on his back at the time of his departure from Mada'in, although the Muslims were then victorious and able to gain unlimited spoils of war. This territory had been previously ruled by Anushirvan and Khusrau Partyz, the Sasanian kings, who had kept thousands of slaves, maidservants and musicians.[39]

Marxism does not offer such a simplistic theory applicable to individual cases. On the contrary, it was Engels who critically discussed Feuerbach's claim that man thinks differently in a palace and in a hut.[40] It is obvious to Marxists that some individuals transcend their class-bound consciousness. The best example is Engels himself, who identified with the working class although he came from a wealthy capitalist family. Mutahhari has failed to assess the probable usefulness of Marxism to explain the early history of Islam. In my opinion, a great deal, though not all, of this history can be explained by Marxist analysis, just as the contemporary problem of corruption can be so explained. Let us hear Engels's explanation of the historical process: 'Men make their own history, whatever its outcome may be, in that each person follows his own consciously desired end, and it is precisely the resultant of these many wills operating in different directions and of their manifold effects upon the outer world that constitutes history. Thus it is also a question of what the many individuals desire. The will is determined by passion or deliberation. But the levers which immediately determine passion or deliberation are of very different kinds. Partly they may be external objects, partly ideal motives, ambition, "enthusiasm for truth and justice", personal hatred or even purely individual whims of all kinds. But, on the one hand, we have seen that the many individual wills active in history for the most part produce results quite other than those intended—often quite the opposite; that their motives, therefore, in relation to the total result, are likewise of only secondary importance. On the other hand, the further question arises: What driving forces in turn stand behind these motives? What are the historical causes which transform themselves into these motives in the brains of the actors?"[41]

Engels rejected the view that history is a conflict between the noble and the ignoble, with the ignoble always triumphant. The important thing is to discover the driving forces behind the motives. We shall quote Engels again in the interest of clarity and accuracy: 'When, therefore, it is a question of investigating the driving powers which—consciously or unconsciously, and indeed very often unconsciously—lie behind the motives of men who act in history and which constitute the real ultimate driving forces of history, then it is not a question so much of the motives of single individuals, however eminent, as of those motives which set in motion great masses, whole peoples, and again whole classes of the people in each people; and this, too, not momentarily, for the transient flaring up of a straw-fire which quickly dies down, but for a lasting action resulting in a great historical transformation. To ascertain the driving causes which here in the minds of acting masses of their leaders—the so-called great men are reflected as conscious motives, clearly or unclearly, directly or in ideological, even glorified form—that is the only path which can put us on the track of the laws holding sway both in history as a whole and at particular periods and in particular lands. Everything which sets men in motion must go through their minds; but what form it will take in the mind will depend very much upon the circumstance.'[42]

Among the driving forces of history the economic one is the most decisive. More than this neither Engels nor Marx ever claimed. The suggestion that the economic element is the only determining one is a meaningless and senseless twist. 'The economic situation is the basis, but the various elements of the superstructure—political forms of the class struggle and its results, to wit: constitutions established by the victorious class after a successful battle, etc., juridical forms, and even the reflexes of all these actual struggles in the brains of the participants, political, juristic, philosophical theories, religious views and their further development into systems of dogmas—also exercise their influence upon the course of the historical struggles and in many cases preponderate in determining their form. There is an interaction of all these elements in which, amidst all the endless host of accidents (that is, of things and events whose inner interconnection is so remote or so impossible of proof that we can regard it as non-existent, as negligible), the economic movement finally asserts itself as necessary.'[43]

It is clear from the above that Engels did not discount the influence of idealized motives, but these motives, in order to transform society, have to appeal to the general economic interest in the sense of needs and control of the mode of production. This interest is thus a powerful stimulus to activity. But the form of activity arising as a reaction to that interest is conditioned by this interest. The truth is that the genesis of a historical ideal in the life of the individual can only be explained ultimately by recourse to the factor of the human type. External historical circumstances only explain the form and outcome in historical experience.

Insensitivity to the values of morality, justice and human dignity has persisted throughout history in different social and economic contexts. The same can be said of the opposite trend. The choice of affiliation is conditioned by the human type. It is a different exercise altogether to explain the genesis of the type. For our purpose it is appropriate to take that as given in each historical context. In other words, when we assess a given historical context such as that of contemporary Singapore and its neighbouring ASEAN countries, we should ask not only what is the social and economic background but also what type of leaders are in power, the negative or positive, the corruptible or the incorruptible.

The interplay of class relations, be it in the nature of conscious conflict or not, is conditioned by the type involved in the encounter. Influences emanating from the type are as deserving of analytic attention as the general social and economic background with its social structure and class relations. To confine analysis to Marxist elements is not adequate. One must extend it to the human type element, focusing attention on the historical ideal. Only then will the analysis be comprehensive.

Endnotes

1. Karl Marx and Frederick Engels, *Collected Works*, Progress Publishers, Moscow, 1979, vol. 11, pp. 602–3. From the *People's Paper*, no. 24, 16 October 1852.

2. *Ibid.*, p. 603.

3. *Ibid.*

4. *Ibid.*

5. *Ibid.*, pp. 345–6. From the article 'Corruption at Elections', *New York Daily Tribune*, 4 September 1852.

6. *Report of the Committee on the Prevention of Corruption*, Ministry of Home Affairs, Government of India, New Delhi, n.d., p. 6.

7. *Ibid.*, pp. 6–7.

8. *Ibid.*, pp. 7–8.

9. *Ibid.*, pp. 9–10.

10. *Ibid.*, p. 10.

11. *Ibid.*, pp. 11–12.

12. *Ibid.*, p. 12.

13. *Ibid.*, p. 200.

14. Syed Hussein Alatas, 'Moral Awakening Needed to End Corruption in Asia', *The Asian Wall Street Journal*, Hong Kong, 25 February 1981. Further on the

effects of tidal corruption see Syed Hussein Alatas, *The Problem of Corruption*, Times Books International, Singapore, 1986.

15. J. Huizinga, *Men and Ideas*, tr. J. S. Holmes and H. van Marle, Meridian Books, New York, 1959, p. 80.

16. *Ibid.*, p. 79.

17. *Ibid.*, p. 80.

18. Shaykh Muhammad Jawad Mughniyyah, *The Despotic Rulers*, tr. M. Fazal Haq, Islamic Seminary Publications, Karachi, 1985, pp. 110–11.

19. Murtada Mutahhari, *Polarization around the Character of Ali Ibn Abi Talib*, tr. from Persian, World Organization for Islamic Services, Tehran, 1981, pp. 14–15.

20. Ibn Khallikan, *Wafayat al-A'yan wa Anba' Abna' al-Zaman*, tr. into French by Mac Guckin de Slane, 1871; reprint ed., Librairie du Liban, Beirut, 1970, vol. 4, pp. 293–4.

21. Syed Razi, comp., *Nahjul Balagha*, English translation, Ansariyan Publications, Qum, Iran, 1981, sermon 198, p. 344.

22. Mr Teh Cheang Wan, Minister for National Development, was found dead at his home on 14 December 1986.

23. *Straits Times*, 27 January 1987, p. 11.

24. *Ibid.*

25. *Ibid.*

26. On the sense of shame and the sense of pride in connection with Asian societies, see Syed Hussein Alatas, 'Asia Needs a Strong Sense of Shame', *The Asian Wall Street Journal*, Hong Kong, 2 December 1980, p. 10.

27. S. Rajaratnam, 'Bureaucracy versus Kleptocracy', in *Political Corruption*, Arnold J. Heidenheimer (eds.), Holt, Rheinhart and Winston, New York, 1970, p. 546.

28. Syed Hussein Alatas, 'Asia Needs a Strong Sense of Shame', p. 10.

29. *Ibid.*

30. S. Rajaratnam, *op. cit.*, p. 547.

31. Mikhail Gorbachov, 'On Reorganization and the Party's Personnel Policy', Report of the General Secretary of the CPSU Central Committee, at a plenary meeting of the CPSU Central Committee on 27 January 1987, *Pravda*, no. 18 (mimeographed version), p. 10.

32. *Ibid.*, p. 62.

33. *Ibid.*, pp. 83–4.

34. *Ibid.*, p. 63.

35. On the factors conditioning the spread or elimination of corruption, see Syed Hussein Alatas, *The Problems of Corruption, passim.*

36. For an arresting example of al-Mansur's cruelty see Shaykh Muhammad Jawad Mughniyyah, *op. cit.*, p. 166.

37. Murtada Mutahhari, *Attitude and Conduct of Prophet Muhammad*, tr. H. V. Dastjerdi, Islamic Propagation Organization, Tehran, 1986, p. 18.

38. For a brief account of Abu Dharr's opposition see Taha Husayn, *Al-Fitnah al-Kubra*: Indonesian translation by M. Tohir under the title *Malapetaka Terbesar dalam Sejarah Islam*, Pustaka Jaya, Jakarta, 1985, pp. 220–4. The original source is Ibn Sa'd, *Kitab al-Tabaqat al-Kabir*, vol. 4 edited by Eduard Sachau et al., E. J. Brill, Leiden, 1904–40, p. 219.

39. Murtada Mutahhari, *Attitude and Conduct of Prophet Muhammad*, p. 19.

40. Karl Marx and Frederick Engels, *On Religion*, Progress Publishers, Moscow, 1966, p. 217. From Engels's work 'Ludwig Feuerbach and the End of Classical German Philosophy'.

41. *Ibid.*, p. 227.

42. *Ibid.*, pp. 228–9.

43. See Engels's letter to J. Bloch, 1890, in Lewis E. Feuer, (ed.), *Marx and Engels*, Doubleday, New York, 1959. p. 398.

Chapter 5

CORRUPTION AND THE DESTINY OF ASIA

THE great watersheds in recent history that dramatically changed the course of human progress and development were the American Revolution of 1775 and the French Revolution of 1789. The declaration of the American bills of rights and the rights of man in the French Revolution was a vigorous rebellion against injustice and exploitation that had persisted for centuries. Corruption figured prominently in the mechanism of injustice and exploitation. Where there is a high degree of injustice and exploitation in the social system, there is also a high degree of corruption. There are astonishingly numerous instances from the recent history of Europe (seventeenth–nineteenth centuries) where corruption is featured together with social injustices arising from the political and social system.

In 1860 the great medical hero Semmelweis who pioneered sterilized hand washing resulting in the saving of lives in childbirth, had to deal with an odious form of corruption at a hospital in Budapest. Despite his efforts the mortality of his patients in hospital remained high. He then made a shocking discovery. The ladies in labour were laid upon filthy sheets which were stained with blood and urine. The sheets were accepted as clean by the head nurse from the laundry contractor, whose rate was very low. The washing transaction was apparently only on paper. Semmelweis shoved the dirty sheets under the nose of the chief official and succeeded to protect his patients from the terrible unhygienic conditions they had to endure.[1]

There is a definite correlation between the degree of corruption and social cruelty, i.e. cruelty arising from the system. During the first century BC corruption developed widely in the Roman Empire. Its administrative system partly contributed to the abuse of office by provincial governors because no one could dispute their authority. They could not be removed and could not be brought to justice after being out of office. Cicero's prosecution of Gais Verres (115–43 BC), a former governor of Sicily, was a dramatic turning point. During the trial Verres managed to bribe many of the judges. Cicero succeeded in prosecuting Verres but his punishment was exile, in which he lived in opulence until he was murdered in 43 BC by order of Mark Anthony.[2] Cicero himself had a tragic end. Embroiled in the conflict after the assassination of Julius Caesar against Marc Antony, he was subsequently arrested and killed in 43 BC.

As mentioned earlier, corruption has plagued human history since time immemorial but the attention towards corruption has not developed in increasing succession throughout that time span. From time to time there was a gush of interest but it was not taken up by the powers that prevailed for the simple reason that they were themselves corrupt. In the last two centuries there was greater interest in the subject as far as thinkers and writers were concerned but the big problem was the phenomenon of what sociologists called the cultural lag. It means the retardation in the rate of change of one part of an interrelated socio-cultural complex as against another part, causing strains in the process. An example is the traffic. The increasing rate of motor cars coming on the road is not accompanied by commensurate expansion and extension of the road system. The effect is a social strain, congestion, traffic jams, parking difficulties, tension in driving and so forth. To summarize, it is a belated recognition of a problem. We may refer to it as an intellectual lag. This is what happened to the attention on corruption.

Many serious works on corruption have been written before. In the fourteenth century, the founder of modern sociology and scientific history, Abdel Rahman Ibn Khaldun had raised the problem of corruption in his monumental work on the history of civilization. Ancient Chinese sages had debated on it. So had the Greeks and

Romans. Their attention, however, focused on the injustice and cruelty against man. The new perspective today is its relation to development in addition to injustice and cruelty. Nevertheless this factor of injustice and cruelty is tightly inter-linked with the issue of development.

When a society is inflicted by what has been referred to earlier, i.e. tidal corruption or total system corruption, it cannot develop in the total comprehensive sense. Economic growth and modernization in certain sectors are considered as development. Of late this concept of development has been questioned but for decades the amoral concept of development has been applied and it is still influential now. Studies of development generally exclude the factor of corruption. Among the sociologists that recognized this problem three decades ago is Stanislav Andreski in his book on Africa and Latin America.[3] The negative effects of corruption have persisted and expanded throughout the post-World War II period. Scholars sensitive to corruption from different disciplines, working on different topics, in different countries and at different times, independent of each other, came to the same conclusion on the devastating effect of corruption on the development of human life.

Let us first consider the goals of development that are undermined by corruption. Generally speaking development seeks to improve the condition of living in the most comprehensive way by altering the backward condition holding us back, in all areas of living such as the economic, social, political, cultural and educational.[4] As we have discussed earlier, corruption distorts the political system, debilitates the administration, undermines the interest and welfare of the community, creates negligence, inefficiency and parasitism in the bureaucracy and prevents honest leaders from succeeding.

Corruption has a composite effect spreading throughout the total life of society. It causes the brain drain to the developing societies. The corrupt environment increases psychological stress and demoralizes people. It fosters criminal activity and erodes the judiciary. In a democratic system, it corrodes the respect for the authority when the electoral process is distorted by corruption. Hence the end result is political instability even though it takes time to appear.

A portrayal of the debilitating effect of corruption, which is actually rampant throughout Asia, from a scholar of Kashmir is particularly helpful. Despite the Corruption Prevention Act of 1947, Jammu and Kashmir, the all pervasive corruption had steadily increased, involving a very wide circle of society. 'It has assumed such large proportions and variegated forms that people have come to believe that it is no more possible to get rid of this malaise from public life.'[5] The author correctly suggests a differential cause of corruption. 'Poor salary and social evils of various kinds affect public servants of lower cadre more than of higher; whereas the urge to acquire more wealth, so that one may enjoy a position of respect and status in the society, exists more in officials belonging to higher echelons of administraiton.'[6]

The Act had not helped much, because the victims, being also beneficiaries of corruption, did not complain. The officials responsible for its implementation were biased, and not bold enough to act against those in the higher echelon of administration for fear of the influence they could wield upon them. In the final analysis it was the political protection from the top that allowed corruption to prevail.

The state as a vigorous engine of growth could breakdown with corruption as the decisive factor. Many African states have experienced such a collapse. Writing on Ghana during the 1980s, E. Gyimah-Boadi said that the state had become utterly unreliable as a facilitator of economic development and social welfare and corruption impeded efforts to solve the development problem. Government properties were siphoned by corrupt officials, poorly remunerated and hardpressed by the economic situtation.[7]

The destructive effects of corruption are there staring at us and anyone who cares to see them cannot afford to brush them aside unless he has no social conscience. The persistence of corruption at an astounding scale has induced an attitude of permissiveness towards it. Hence the oblique reference to the non-disastrous role of corruption made from time to time by political leaders and scholars tolerant of corruption. They say that corruption has not prevented economic growth; that development continues; that stability prevails and that the system works. A large area of the non-Western world can be subsumed under this condition.

But the above assessment has a serious flaw. Cruelty, injustice and corruption favour any conditions they can thrive in. When corruption was rampant in the Roman Empire, Rome was strong, growing and developing. The cruelty of the Nazi regime in Germany after it took power in 1933 did not prevent its industrial and economic development so much so it could embark on a war preparation. Who would consider the former Union of the Soviet Socialist Republics (USSR) an under-developed power despite its rampant corruption?

Corruption affects the welfare and well-being of human individuals in society without necessarily blocking economic growth. What it blocks is the development of social and individual justice. Indonesia had been praised for its impressive rate of growth during the Suharto era. So had corruption grown widely and deeply. The government and the state were solidly stable. This brings us to the crux of the problem. If a stable state and government bouyed by some kind of economic growth does not guarantee against corruption but instead generates more and more of it, what then would achieve the non-corrupt situation of governance. The answer is a clean political leadership. One resolve of the leadership of a political party in Singapore clarifies the significant role of leadership in the fight against corruption. In his memoirs, the former Prime Minister of Singapore, Mr Lee Kuan Yew, revealed the thinking of his colleagues on corruption as the decisive factor for the party to contest the 1959 election to form the government rather than to spend another five-year term in the opposition.

They were afraid that if the then government in office, the Singapore People's Alliance were to continue for another term, corruption would spread from the ministers to the civil servants. There would then be no effective administration to implement Mr Lee Kuan Yew's party's policies.[8] Hence a leadership that is serious about the moral condition of the bureaucracy expresses its genuine concern about the problem of corruption.

It is not the political system or the economic condition that is decisive in the elimination of corruption but the nature of the leadership in power. A corrupt leadership would immediately and quickly breed corruption down the line of authority. Once this takes place, it would take decades to change it. One political generation succeeds another with the same dominant traits, corruption.

This is what is happening in the greater parts of Asia. In many parts of Asia the salary of civil servants is insufficient for a month. In the richly endowed part of Asia, i.e. Southeast Asia, with its vast economic potential and impressive natural resources, a most conducive climate to agriculture, and a sizeable educated stratum, the salary of government servants often is enough for about two weeks instead of a month.[9] I have personally witnessed this for almost half a century, since the early 1950s just after World War II.

From a political leadership that could not ensure even a level of salary sufficient for basic needs, for almost half a century, what can be expected? At the same time, during the same period the corrupt increases in wealth by leaps and bounds. The scope and volume of corruption dramatically increased during this period. The history of Asia since World War II is verily the history of corruption. Considering the multifarious effects of corruption in human society, Asia is doomed to lag further and further away from the developed societies of the West. What then is the destiny of Asia?

It seems to me the destiny of Asia is to create another great transformation similar to Europe and America in the eighteenth century. What does this entail? First a colossal mass awakening of the Asian people towards the direction of a social order based on human rights and social justice integrated with the Asian traditions that would ensure the elimination of poverty, corruption, despotism, political thuggery and opportunism, injustice and oppression. The philosophical and intellectual framework has yet to be worked out.

Second, this requires the effort of a group of thinkers to generate and propagate the Asian ideal of social reconstruction similar to what happened during the French Revolution. If the consensus amongst the thinkers is that a democratic system is to be preferred than an authoritarian one, it should not be an imitative version of the Western model. Let it not be forgotten that the current democratic system in the West is a new creation of the West *vis–à–vis* its own political tradition, during the eighteenth century. A similar occurrence should happen in Asia.

Third, in the absence of such generative forces for a new tradition to effectively awaken the Asian masses so that they can condition a new political leadership functioning in the direction of the ideal, unlike the type we have at the moment, permissive or helpless against corruption, despotism and social injustice, recourse should be made to fully utilize the Information Technology (IT) networks and other multi-media outlets by Asian thinkers and others concerned to propagate the ideal of excellence suitable for Asia.

The above are some suggestions for action, not a proposal for a final solution. There are many dimensions to the problem which cannot be discussed in a single book, especially a modest one as the present book. Even a lifetime cannot be sufficient to deal conclusively with an issue such as corruption. The intention here is to awaken serious interest in the subject in the hope that more and more effort will be done to eliminate this most devastating scourge in human history, corruption, together with its related antecedents and causes.

He who ignores the problem of corruption, ignores the problem of evil. He who ignores the problem of evil, assists in the development of evil. He who assists in the development of evil, is part of the universe of evil. No human being wants evil, anywhere at any time. If only those in power would realize this, by demonstration, not enunciation.

Endnotes

1. Howard W. Haggard, *Devils, Drugs and Doctors*, Pocket Books, New York, 1959, pp. 86–7.

2. Syed Hussein Alatas, *Corruption: Its Nature, Causes and Functions*, Gower Publishing Company, Aldershot, England, Brookfield, USA, 1990, p. 17.

3. Stanislav Andreski, *Parasitism and Subversion*, Weidenfeld and Nicolson, London, 1966 and *The African Predicament*, Michael Joseph, London, 1968.

4. For the characteristics of backwardness, at least thirty can be cited. See Appendix, 'The Ideal of Excellence', p. 137 of this book.

5. Kulwant Singh, 'The Working of Jammu and Kashmir Prevention of Corruption Acts: An Empirical Study', *Journal of the Indian Law Institute, 1987, vol. 29:3,* p. 408.

6. *Ibid.*

7. E. Gyimah-Boadi, in Thandika Mkandawire and Adebayo Olukoshi (eds.), *Between Liberalisation and Oppression*, Codesria, Dakar, Senegal, 1995, pp. 219, 222.

8. Memoirs of Lee Kuan Yew, *The Singapore Story*, Times Editions, Singapore, 1998, p. 293.

9. Djamester A. Simarmata, *Reformasi Ekonomi Menurut Undang-Undang Dasar 1945*, Centre for Policy and Implementation Studies, Jakarta, 1998, p. 29.

APPENDICES

Appendix A

The Ideal of Excellence
(*Lecture given by Dr Syed Hussein Alatas, University of Singapore, at the Asian Youth Council 4th Advanced Youth Leadership Training Workshop, 28 May – 9 June 1978, National Youth Training Institute, Singapore*)

When it was suggested to me that I deliver this lecture to you on some issues of social development in Asian countries, my immediate reaction was to search for the most relevant theme concerning contemporary Asia. I shall speak here of non-Communist Asia. I do not have sufficient information on the Communist countries of Asia. I have also not had the opportunity to visit any of them. Hence I have no first hand knowledge of the conditions there.

My view on the political system is shared by many in Asia who happen to be in the awkward position of dissent with the dominant trend in Asia as well as the alternative suggested by Communism or that uncritical and imitative blend of neo-Marxism currently being imported is dominated by a vulgar feudal–capitalist trend whose exploitative nature is not to be found in the present advanced liberal–capitalist society of the West.

The feudal–capitalism of the greater part of Asia is so ruthless and exploitative that it makes even Western capitalists shudder. What I shall be discussing here is not the political and social system Asia should have. I would like to discuss something more basic than this. In order to have the right system, we should have the will to achieve it.

From human history we learn that a social and political system emerges as the result of the effort of thinkers. Before their effort crystallized into distinctly articulated thought systems, these men and women were moved by certain impulses and sentiments around certain values and ideals. It is this I shall discuss in this lecture today. I shall call these ideas and values the ideal of excellence. This ideal of excellence is supported by two significant components, the sense of pride, and the sense of shame. It is these components which are sadly lacking in the collective life of Asia.

My interest in this problem was awakened during the war, in Java, when I was about fourteen years of age. During the period of our youth, my contemporaries and I went through a major transition period. We have witnessed life under colonial rule, under Japanese occupation, and now under our own independent government. Despite all these changes, one thing

137

practically remains the same for the greater part of Asia. The ideal of excellence has not seized the minds and hearts of the groups in power and other significant groups in society.

What is this ideal of excellence we should be concerned about? It is the conception of a decent, just, and dignified life for the Asian people. Do we see in the greater part of Asia now a decent, just and dignified life among the people? Anyone who claims that he sees it is blind. What do we see instead? Misery, backwardness, exploitation, ignorance, and disrespect for the dignity of the human individual.

Scholars of development have characterized the conditions in Asia and the rest of the Third World by the following:

(1)   a very high proportion of the population in agriculture, usually some 70 to 90 per cent;
(2)   considerable disguised unemployment;
(3)   lack of employment outside agriculture;
(4)   very little capital per head;
(5)   low income per head;
(6)   practically no saving for the large mass of the people;
(7)   savings most often are of those classes whose values are not conducive to commerce or industry;
(8)   output in agriculture mostly of cereals and primary raw materials;
(9)   a major proportion of expenditures on food and necessities;
(10)   the main exports are foodstuffs and raw materials;
(11)   a low volume of trade and productivity per capita;
(12)   poor credit and marketing facilities;
(13)   poor housing;
(14)   low yields per acre;
(15)   a general weakness or absence of a middle class;
(16)   insufficient educational facilities;
(17)   inadequate communication and transport facilities;
(18)   underdeveloped technology;
(19)   high fertility rate;
(20)   high mortality rate;
(21)   low life expectancy;
(22)   inadequate nutrition;
(23)   lack of hygiene, public health and sanitation; and
(24)   a high rate of illiteracy.

To the above listed by development scholars may be added the following:
(25)   the absence of a social demand for science amongst the bulk of the population;

(26)   the prevalence of magic and superstition amongst all groups;
(27)   corruption in high and low places;
(28)   lack of organizational efficiency;
(29)   lack of maintenance mentality; and
(30)   the absence of an effectively functioning group of thinkers to awaken public interest in social-justice and problem solving.[1]

The above list can be further extended, such as the prevalence of a negative imitative mentality amongst the educated elites, and the lack of a social conscience which brings us back to the ideal of excellence. Many of the characteristics listed should awaken in us a sense of shame. It is this absence of the sense of shame which has brought about the situation of little success in development effort despite the fact that the topic has been noisily proclaimed by political leaders throughout Asia and the Third World. There is hardly any noble aim which has escaped the utterances of these leaders.

Let me now present to you a concrete instance of what I mean by the sense of shame. Recently, during my holiday, I attended a religious conference, in the capital of a Southeast Asian country. On the way back to the airport I asked the taxi driver how much he earned. He told me that his total income was about US$150 per month. 'Not bad', I said to myself. Then I became more curious. I asked him how long did he work daily. He replied: 'Twenty-four hours!' I said to myself: 'This is impossible!' I then asked him how he managed to work 24 hours every alternate day. He started at eight in the morning, until the next day. Then he was free for 24 hours.

The transport service belonged to some high dignitaries of the armed forces. Each driver would drive back and forth to the airport for about seven or eight times in 24 hours. If I were to estimate on a minimum basis, that is one passenger per trip, we would arrive at fifteen trips per driver in 24 hours. The total fare for fifteen trips would be US$30. The driver was paid US$5 for his effort. If the company would consider the normal and human working hours for our glorious and spiritual Asia as eight, it would have to employ three drivers to keep the taxi in service for 24 hours. Instead it employed only two drivers for one taxi, which means that each driver works for 12 hours on a daily average for the month.

The greed of the company prevented it from employing an additional driver. Look what it does to the existing drivers. The sleep pattern is distorted. They sleep off and on between trips, sometimes for half an hour, sometimes for three hours. On the other hand on the following day they have the time to sleep. Would it be possible to maintain a consistent sleep pattern in such an alternating situation? I doubt it.

I was told there were numerous drivers working in 24 hours shifts. At the very worst, if each driver brings in a total payment of US$30 per day, the total would be in the region of US$450 per driver, per month, working for 15 days each. If we subtract US$150 for the driver, the company receives US$300 per month from one driver. Since two drivers use one car each for 24 hours throughout the month, the company would receive about US$600 from each car. Within one and a half years it could recover the cost of the car.

Presumably the company obtained the cars on credit. It is indeed a profitable business but who bears the main brunt of the undertaking? It is the drivers and yet they were unscrupulously exploited having to work for 24 hours at a stretch. What comes up in my mind is the question, how could such an exploitation prevail? This prevails because there is an absence of the social conscience, there is no sense of shame, there is no ideal of excellence governing the behaviour of the ruling power or those influential members of society.

Life goes on as usual in many capitals of Asia. The academics, the civil servants, the politicians, the businessmen, the journalists, the lawyers, the physicians, the teachers, meet in parties and conferences and conduct pleasant conversations and discussions. Rarely is social injustice tackled as a serious subject. The youths are inducted into the system without realizing that the process evades the awakening of the social conscience. The ideal of excellence is relegated into the background.

The gigantic ideological machine of the negative establishment quietly grinds the ideal of excellence into fragmented bits and pieces. One is not encouraged to steal. Ah! But this is only from the individual. It is all right to steal from the public, from the government and from business organizations, by way of corruption. In the ultimate analysis corruption may take the form of either theft or extortion. Money or property changes hands in a manner prejudicial to public interest.

Corruption, which has been the scourge of Asian societies, is slowly being accorded a place in the scheme of things. There is a growing tendency amongst Asians to consider corruption as an Asian way of life. This idea is promoted by those who are against the ideal of excellence. If a society accepts corruption as a way of life, it is a sure sign of spiritual and cultural breakdown. That which is dangerous and destructive should not be made acceptable.

The ideal of excellence which should prevail in a community should lead to an aversion towards corruption, social injustice, diseases, poverty, hunger, ignorance, loss of self-respect, and all the other evils of human social life. We should also recognize the role played by those who are leading the community towards the ideal of excellence. This should not be confined to verbal expressions, but also to the explanation of historical events.

Those who relegated the ideal of excellence to the background are prone to explain events in the structural and situational manner. They eliminated the role of human leadership motivated by the ideal of excellence. No credit is given to the type of men that strive for the ideal of excellence. An instance at hand is the explanation on the development of Singapore. The fact that Singapore has succeeded to improve the standard of living, the social organization, the quality of life of its citizens and residents, is attributed to the small size of the island.

The main cause is suggested to be the size, not the people of Singapore and their leaders. I have often heard this argument during the last ten years. In discussions on this topic, I had always argued that the size of a country is a secondary factor. If the earlier political party were to remain in power, Singapore would have been different. Singapore under colonial rule had slum areas, relatively little industry, and greater disparity in income. There was corruption in government circles. The streets, the canals, the stalls and the market place were not as clean as they are now. The size of Singapore then was not bigger than it is now.

It would have been much easier to regulate everything then since there was also a smaller population. The size of Singapore had nothing to do with the determination of the authority to plant trees, to stop people from spitting in public, to eliminate floods, to have a clean government, and to have a system of handling industrial relation, etc. As a sociologist, I would be the last to deny the influence of size and other external factors. But what is more decisive is the influence of the leadership and the people's perception of their role, in the effort to approach the ideal of excellence.

My favourite argument against those who want to play down the role of the leadership is to invite them to compare Singapore with a city of comparable size, taking items which are not negatively influenced by the hinterland, such as public spitting and littering the streets. The absence of a hinterland is actually a source of some added problems. There are several cities of Asia of comparable size. I maintain that if those in power in that city are determined to keep the streets clean and to plant trees, they could do so, given comparable conditions of climate and demography.

During my student days in the Netherlands following World War II, it was a very clean country. The cities of Holland were bigger than many in Asia that were not clean. Size is not a factor at all. I do not wish to simplify issues by saying that everything depends on the leadership. All I wish to say is that the leadership of a society is the most decisive element in the network of causes governing the development or ruin of that society.

It is crucial that society's leadership is swayed by the ideal of excellence, having the right sense of shame as well as pride. If the leadership of society manifested the sense of shame of backwardness and exploitation, this will spread amongst the population, eventually building the foundation of a permanent attitude which could then sustain a prolonged effort at right action, involving patience, sacrifice and understanding.

I have mentioned the planting of trees and keeping the streets clean merely as convenient illustrations. There are many other significant achievements affecting public welfare, such as the functioning of the Wages Council and housing development. It is not my intention here to conduct a survey of achievements of the Singapore society and its leadership. All I want to emphasize is that it does make a great deal of difference whether society is led by people swayed by the ideal of excellence or not.

If you ask me what is the most important problem of development, without any hesitation, my answer is, the leadership. The rest are less crucial compared to this. If we have a bad economic system, it can be changed, but for this we need a leadership that perceives the need for change and is able to formulate and execute the alternative. If we have unemployment, the condition can be improved, but for this we need a leadership that is able to assess the problem and plan for its solution.

A creative leadership swayed by the ideal of excellence is like a gardener. He will eventually find the right soil and the right crop for society's need. The system and planning for the cultivation is no doubt important but the factor of the gardener is very crucial. In the last few decades the Asian countries have had all sorts of development plans which are sound in themselves. But these plans are eventually distorted in the process of implementation particularly by a leadership who was not serious about development.

If we want to act really as responsible human beings, we have to adopt the correct attitude towards problem solving. The more difficult the problem, the more attention it deserves. It is easier for society to acquire a good development plan than to generate a good leadership. In the present context of our history, it is not the plans that are difficult to come by, but a good leadership. Hence more attention should be given to this, and it is certainly a much more difficult problem.

How do we generate the right kind of leadership if we were not to leave it to the accident of history? Generating a good leadership is not like formulating development plans where it requires research and meetings of experts. It is not like training a professional either. The way to generate a good leadership is for everyone concerned to promote the ideal of excellence in their different walks of life by intensive attitude building and advocacy of the moral and intellectual issues that envelop the ideal of excellence.

The moment the ideal of excellence becomes a collective demand, leaders will emerge that answer the requirement. On the other hand, if the opposite prevails, that is the ideal of decadence governing the collective life of society, another type of leadership conforming to it will emerge. Society gets the leaders they deserve but at certain situations in history leaders have been thrown out of power while in other situations oppressive and indolent leaders succeed to maintain a long period of control. Whatever is the historical mechanism the fact remains that at the bottom of every great change, there is the intense will to have something better, there is a heightening sense of shame, there is a sharpening of the social conscience.

I believe it is the most solemn mission of the youths of Asia to awaken this will to change for the better, to propagate the need for a moral and creative leadership, and to apply the intellectual power to understand and solve issues. During their exposure to policy discourses, let them remember the type of man needed to generate and carry through the policy. Striving for the ideal of excellence is like building a house.

In the entire process of building several stages have to be passed. It is the current practice to discuss only the second stage, not the first and the last. What is given the most attention is the design of the house. What about those who will ultimately do the work of construction? More important still, what about the man himself? Does he badly want the house? If he badly wants the house, it follows that he should carefully get the right design and the right workers to construct the house. If he only talks loudly about the design and is not really serious about having the house or who are going to construct it, then we can be sure that it will never be built.

People have to be extremely serious about achieving the ideal of excellence. Then they can go into the question of plans and policy. Then they can carefully think about the implementers. Seriousness of purpose is the ultimate foundation of human progress. Without this foundation only the opposite will take its place. My practical suggestion to the youths of Asia is to pay more attention to the problem of injustice and the ways and means to overcome it. We have to study, amongst others, the social system operating in a certain society; the nature and function of its ruling class; the degree of public awareness and aspiration; the forms and manifestations of injustice; the nature of the economic relation; the functioning of the rule of law; the level of scientific and technological attainment; and finally, the best manner to bring about change and the kind of leadership required.

Courses, seminars and workshops, dealing with the role of youths, with policies and plans at improving conditions, if isolated from the above issues, may function as an ideological device to divert the attention of the youths away from basic problems the ruling classes do not wish to solve, just as religious teachings have been used in that manner for several centuries. The spiritual development of the individual has been highlighted and cut off from his social and economic development by religious leaders who unwittingly allow injustice and exploitation to prevail, owing to their silence on the subject.

The generation of a genuine consciousness of the problems facing Asian societies is the first requisite of change to the better. If this is not done through existing formal channels, then the informal channels should be used. A new interest has to be created amongst youths in significant topics for reflection and conversation. They should not confine their orbit of interest to the trivial and the digressive. They should be able to locate their activities in the scheme of things. They should ask themselves whether their activities really help to make Asia a better place to live in. They should ask themselves whether it is a disgrace to have a ruling class plundering the wealth of the country for their own decadent and selfish ends, under the guise of nationalism, religion, or public welfare.

Endnote

1. On this issue see Syed Hussein Alatas, *Intellectuals in Developing Societies*, Frank Cass, London, 1977.

A p p e n d i x B

Moral Awakening Needed to End Corruption in Asia
(Extract of an article by Prof. Syed Hussein Alatas in The Asian Wall Street Journal, Hong Kong, 25 February 1981)

No society can be completely free of petty, isolated corruption. But that is not a crucial problem. The real concern must be about 'tidal' corruption that floods the entire state apparatus, including those at the centre of power. Like a tide, this practice rises to immerse everything in its path.

This tidal corruption multiplies the number of perpetrators of the illegal practice more rapidly than other types of criminal behaviour. By so doing it increases the dangerous and unhealthy elements of society at a pace too fast to be controlled by the forces of law. More and more people become criminals. It paralyses the administrative machinery and dampens the enthusiasm of sincere and capable public officials. And it can lead to serious neglect of the people's welfare.

Ultimately, widespread corruption will spark bitterness that can result in a crisis or even revolution and civil war.

Often tidal corruption starts among the top officials and businessmen. As prices rise and administration becomes chaotic, lower ranking government officials adopt the practice in an effort to maintain their livelihood. So the economic difficulties for the lower officials and their subsequent involvement in corruption are caused by the corruption that starts at the top. It is sometimes argued that businessmen have to get involved in corruption in Asia because it is the only way to get anything done. But if a shop was to try to operate in a street controlled by an extortion syndicate, few of these businessmen would argue that extortion should be paid, even though it had become a condition for the shop to function.

Certainly, corruption can favour an individual business that profits from it. But its influence on business as a whole is deleterious. For each who benefits, there are hundreds who suffer. In a corrupt business environment, competition no longer is based on quality, efficiency or other market influences so that the economy becomes increasingly distorted.

The billions of dollars drained off by corruption in recent years could have been used for legitimate government and business purposes. More honest administrative and business communities could have greatly enhanced productivity and effectiveness.

Governments, of course, can act against corruption with proper laws and enforcement agencies. Sources of corruption in the administration can be identified. Administrative practices that tend to breed corruption, such as those that create bottlenecks, long queues for permits and systems of tenders with loopholes for corruption can be reformed.

But that is not adequate. The other method to combat tidal corruption is the generation of counter tidal wave against corruption. This approach involves the rise of a powerful anti-corruption mentality among the public to such an extent that it sways the government. It is the only approach that can offer real hope in Asia. Relying on government-initiated action is unlikely to succeed for the simple reason that it presupposes the existence of the powerful will of an honest government. Such a government, as a collectivity, rarely can be found in Asia. Indeed this programmatic method of preventing corruption has largely failed in many Third World countries, including those in West, South and Southeast Asia.

Some state leaders are not personally corrupt but they tolerate the corruption surrounding them. Their pillars of power are corrupt party stalwarts. These governments sometimes have anti-corruption units that have themselves become sources of corruption. In some countries these units function as window dressing, tracking down minor cases of corruption, or they serve as a political tool to discredit threatening rivals in the power struggle. Often also they have no independent status but are controlled by the group in power.

So the crucial changes that are needed go further than just changes in personalities and parties in power. These changes require a tremendous effort, preceded by a profound moral awakening, imbued with an ideal of excellence and moved by a sense of shame at the poverty, exploitation, callousness and moral ambiguity that now prevail in much of Asia.

Appendix C

(An extract from Wafaqi Mohtasib (Ombudsman) Sardar Muhammad Iqbal's Annual Report for 1983, Government of Pakistan)

There is no dearth of talk about corruption which, no doubt, exists. However, it may be noted that the real victim of corruption is often the government itself. Both the corrupter and the corrupted benefit from this nefarious practice. Understandably the beneficiaries are reluctant to lodge complaints which partly explains why only a small number of concrete complaints have been made about corruption. It would be interesting to observe that in the majority of cases where allegations of corruption have been levelled, we have not been receiving any reply on return call for confirmation.

There is no doubt whatsoever about the compulsive need to excise the cancer of corruption from our society. The phenomenon of bureaucratic corruption has been existing for a long time. To hope for its complete elimination overnight would be, however, idealistic. A pragmatic approach is, therefore, indicated concentrating in the first instance on reducing the incidence and arresting the trends of corruption.

The improvement of governmental procedures, in this connection, among other things, would go a long way in improving the situation. Adoption of scientific management-methods including computerisation can prove quite helpful. A very high priority needs to be accorded to avoidance of administrative delays which indeed constitutes the main source of corruption.

Appendix D

(*Extract from the Wafaqi Mohtasib (Ombudsman) Sadar Muhammad Iqbal's Annual Report for 1985, Government of Pakistan*)

Corruption is an evil which should be fought by all of us. It is a cancer which can be excised only by the efforts of every member of the society. For any penny which is paid, there is one who gives and one who takes. To be candid, I have seen that many people talk about corruption but never, for their own reasons, try to make an earnest effort to fight it. Corruption, in many cases has become a participatory venture where both the giver and the taker benefit. The only loser is the state. Unless one learns to sacrifice narrow interests and wage a crusade against corruption, this evil will not only persist but will assume progressively alarming proportions.

Of course most of us do not want to be accessory to this nefarious practice. We should, therefore, resist the extortionist demands of the dishonest public servants. The best way to fight corruption as well as other forms of injustice is not to keep silent but to bring such cases boldly and fearlessly to the notice of the concerned authorities. One may say that this is easier said than done; that complaining might invite further odium of the powers-that-be; that wrath or vengefulness on the part of the agencies could mar the very future of the complaining citizens. There would be some truth in that. But there is also truth in the fact that no error or wrong can be rectified unless people fearlessly seek its redressal.

There have been many efforts to study the phenomenon of bureaucratic corruption. A plethora of committees and commissions had been given the task to identify its causes and suggest remedies. A bewildering variety of institutions have been set up from time to time for eradication of corruption. Notwithstanding all these endeavours, the incidence of corrupt practices has been increasing. It is true that corruption can only be eradicated through a comprehensive strategy covering various facets—social, economic and administrative. But I feel that in our preoccupation with the grand strategy and design, we have not been able to make much progress on the ground. This is so because a large number of elements are involved in the process. It is exceedingly difficult to implement various components of the strategy at the right time and with the right speed.

My advice is that along with thinking out comprehensive solutions, we may start with only one concrete measure, namely, making our government officers accessible to the people. The government functionaries should make it a point to open their offices to the people every day without exception and should also maintain an effective liaison with their subordinate staff. Meeting with people will keep the senior officers constantly aware of grievances of the citizen. It will make possible for them to take immediate action and give directions. This should prove very efficacious in regard to matters on which the subordinate functionaries would be sitting on files for corrupt motives. It is my considered view that accessibility alone will bring about a minor revolution. But accessibility will have to be ensured in actual fact, on the ground. It would mean an officer spending half an hour or so daily in meeting with the aggrieved citizens. One possible reaction is that the time for this purpose is not available and important government work would suffer. It should be, however, realized that the most important work of the government is to satisfy the citizens. The government exists for the people and not vice versa. This daily expenditure of time is a very small cost to pay for ensuring probity and responsiveness of the governmental machinery.

* * *

Corruption is one of the many causes of injustice. It is a significant factor but it is not the sole element underlying administrative injustice. Till the establishment of the institution of Ombudsman in Pakistan, injustice perpetrated through causes other than corruption received scant attention. No grievance redressal mechanism (save courts operating under jurisdictional and operational constraints) existed in respect of acts which were arbitrary, unreasonable, biased, unfair, discriminatory and negligent. Similarly, cases of delay, inattention, incompetence, inefficiency, ineptitude, improper exercise of discretion and arrogance were not open to the scrutiny of any independent organisation. Attempts were only made, though without any marked success, to look into cases of injustice stemming from corruption. But the accent in the process was on apprehending and punishing the guilty functionaries. Redressal of the citizen's grievance was only secondary and incidental. This state of affairs left the citizen, to a large measure, defenceless against administrative injustice. The setting up of the institution of Ombudsman thus removed a critical institutional gap.

* * *

Taking all those facts into consideration, the increasing menace of bureaucratic corruption has convinced me about the need for a more active role by the institution of Ombudsman. This would involve imparting a new

149

dimension to our conceptual and operational framework and would represent a point of departure from the functions of the Ombudsman performed elsewhere in the world. I have desisted from making this proposal earlier as I wanted to consolidate our core function of grievance-redressal. Now a stage has come for making a qualitative change in the role of this institution. I recommend that all the Anti-Corruption Agencies of the Federal Government may be placed under the direct supervision and operational command of the *Wafaqi Mohtasib*. The major reason for the failure of these agencies has been their lack of operational independence of the executive. This institution with its changed role will have to be given additional staff and resources so that attention commensurate to the importance of this aspect of work can be given. Anti-corruption operations under this scheme will be carried on in a co-ordinated manner without any fear or favour under the supervision and control of the *Mohtasib*—a functionary truly independent of the executive. The process of eradication of corruption will not only be characterized by impartiality but will also enjoy public confidence which is indeed a crucial ingredient for success.

Appendix E

'Halt Graft with Vigilance Group'
(*Extract of an article which appeared in the New Straits Times, Kuala Lumpur, 12 September 1983.*)

Johore Baru, Sun—The government has been urged to set up a vigilance committee empowered to investigate and keep tabs on corruption in the different government agencies, departments and ministries.

Such a high-powered committee, comprising retired people like judges and other dedicated public servants will be an effective watchdog for the government in its fight against corruption in the country.

Speaking to reporters during a dialogue session on the Problems of Corruption Throughout History, the head of Malay Studies at the Singapore National University, Prof Syed Hussein Alatas, said the other factor was a need for the Anti-Corruption Agency to put up an annual report on its activities, including its size, budget, manpower.

'By doing so the public would have more confidence in the agency and subsequently be willing to come forward to help the agency fight corruption more effectively,' he said.

Prof Syed Hussein who returned recently after a one-year fellowship at the International Center for Scholars, Woodrow Wilson Center Smithsonian Institution in Washington, DC, said in his research on corruption, he found these two factors missing in our government's fight against corruption.

'The Indian government, due to the extent of corruption in that country, set up a vigilance committee about 10 years ago to alert the government on corrupt practice.

'Our government too can do it, and once it is done, the public will feel the government show concern, but the committee mustn't be turned into a political gimmick,' he said.

He said the committee could comprise about 10 high calibre persons, and have access to all government departments, agencies and the like just like the Accountant-General's Department.

Prof Syed Hussein further contended that the committee by virtue of its role, would be in a better position to introduce institutional safeguards and other preventive measures so that in stages, the growth of corruption could be prevented.

'As the committee's functions and role will be routine, there will be no reason for any ministry, department or statutory body to feel slighted or embarrassed,' he said, adding that the existence of the committee would be more of a 'deterrent' to all.

'While the ACA is doing a fine job, its role is confined more to investigations and prosecuting but it is not able to introduce preventive measures against corruption,' he said.

He pointed out that the public could also help the committee by writing in about corrupt practices or other problems they might have encountered.

On the need for ACA to prepare annual reports, made available to the public, Prof Syed Hussein said this was being done in Hong Kong.

'We are not expecting an identification but at least we, the public, will be in a position to know what's going on.'

He said at the moment, the public was not given a clear picture of what the ACA was doing other than occasional reports in the newspapers about investigations and arrests.

'It's like a patient who is not informed about his disease by the doctor—the public must be told what the ACA has done for the whole year, its shortcomings, problems and difficulties,' he said.

Appendix F

White Paper on What Led to the Scandal.
(Extracts of an article which appeared in the New Straits Times, Kuala Lumpur, 12 March 1986)

The White Paper on the Bumiputra Malaysia Finance (BMF) affair said fraud, malpractice and shortcomings in supervision and control led to the RM2.5 million loans scandal.

It said the scandal resulted from malpractice, mismanagement and neglect to adhere to banking procedures on the part of members of the board of directors as well as senior officials of Bank Bumiputra Malaysia Berhad (BBMB) and BMF who were motivated by self-interest.

The paper outlined incidents of fraud and manipulation which took place between 19 December 1979 and 12 October 1982, by members of the board and officials of BMF who were in league with the Carrian Group and those connected with George Tan.

These incidents included a so-called 'concerted plan' involving loans totalling US$292 million (about RM2,136 billion) to Carrian-owned companies for the purpose of speculation in the stock market and in real estate.

The paper, tabled in Dewan Rakyat yesterday, said the loans were approved as market and/or term loans to conceal their real purpose.

They were given out to companies that had not been formed and to those with a paid-up capital of only HK$2 (60 sen). They were also granted without official approval of the board of directors, by verbal approval, and to companies closely linked to the members of the board of directors and or BMF officials.

The paper said the BMF Committee of Enquiry which was headed by Auditor-General Tan Sri Ahmad Noordin Zakaria regarded these incidents to be prompted by intention to defraud.

It also listed 15 incidents of malpractice and/or deviation from normal and prudent banking practices accepted by the banking community.

Among such malpractices the committee uncovered was the existence of a 'retirement fund' for BMF local staff in Hong Kong with a gift of two million Carrian Investment Ltd. shares from George Tan.

Members of the board of directors, the management and BMF staff all profited from their relationship with the Carrian Group.

* * *

Among the malpractice which occurred were approval of loans without a complete credit analysis, approval before any application was made, approval to yet-to-be formed companies and approval of large sums to companies with a paid-up capital of only HK$2 (60 sen).

Other malpractices were:

* Loans and advances approved without proper or adequate collateral;
* Loans approved based on collateral in the form of post-dated cheques;
* Loans approved as money market loans to non-financial institutions to conceal their real purpose;
* Acceptance of a personal guarantee from George Tan for US$500 million (about RM1.225 billion) without an analysis of the net worth of his assets; and
* Names of borrowers changed without permission.

BMF was also said to have submitted a report saying loans to the Carrian Group had been reduced, whereas this was not true. In fact, the loans were transferred to companies outside the group but which were connected to it.

On the weaknesses in supervision and control by BBMB, the paper said several members of the BBMB board of directors and management had obstructed efforts to impose effective supervisory and regulatory measures on BMF.

It said they did this out of self-interest as they were also members of the BMF board of directors.

This was carried further when they were also appointed to the supervisory committee and consequently the malpractice and activities of the BMF board of directors continued without any restriction.

Appendix G

Laws Alone 'Cannot Curb Mismanagement'
(An article which appeared in The Straits Times, Singapore, 13 March 1986.)

Kuala Lumpur, Wed.—The Bumiputra Malaysia Finance (BMF) Committee of Enquiry said in its final report that legal controls do not in themselves ensure a healthy business climate and public confidence in corporate management.

It described personal quality and integrity of people entrusted with the responsibility of controlling and managing corporations on behalf of the shareholders and depositors as even more important.

Constant attention should also be given to the need for ensuring that adequate checks and balances, particularly in the banking industry, were carried out, the report said.

'Any system of internal control in existence needs to be reviewed from time to time to ensure that it works in practice,' it added.

The committee noted that in recent years, various amendments had been made to the Banking Act and the Companies Act in an effort to inculcate a higher sense of discipline, standard of accountability and public morality in corporate business and banking.

'These amendments may have been influenced to a large extent by the lessons learnt from the BMF scandal and other business failures due to mismanagement and abuse of powers,' the committee said.

The committee said that when wrong doings were discovered, firm and positive action should be taken to remedy the situation.

'Those responsible should be removed from positions of management and not be permitted to continue, as in the case of the BMF.'

The committee said irregularities and crimes, such as those it had recounted, occurred because of failings in the system or in the individuals who operated it.

'We do not consider that there were failings in the Malaysian banking system. Conventional banking procedures and controls existed and were generally used satisfactorily by those concerned.'

But, it added, in the cases reported by the committee, the individuals involved—including some at the very top of the system—had failed to take the appropriate control measures when they discovered at least a part of what was going wrong.—Bernama.

BIBLIOGRAPHY

Abdul Qayyum, *Letters of Al-Ghazzali*, Islamic Publications, Lahore, 1976.

Abdullah Yusuf Ali (tr. ed.), *The Holy Quran*, Ashraf, Lahore, 1938 (3 vols.).

Allamah Shibli Nu'mani, *Umar the Great*, tr. Maulana Zafar Ali Khan, Ashraf Publications, Lahore, 1947.

Amanat Presiden Soeharto dalam Sidang Kabinet Paripurna 31 Djanuari 1970, Djakarta, Departemen Penerangan Republik Indonesia, Djakarta, 1970.

Andreski, Stanislav, *Parasitism and Subversion*, Weidenfeld and Nicolson, London, 1966.

——, *The African Predicament*, Michael Joseph, London, 1968.

The Asian Wall Street Journal, Hong Kong, 31 March 1986.

Asiaweek, Hong Kong, 13 July 1984.

Azam, M. A., *The Anatomy of Corruption*, Society for Pakistan Studies, Dacca, 1970.

Bailey, D. H. 'The Effects of Corruption in a Developing Nation', *The Western Political Quarterly*' December 1966, vol. 19.

Bary, W. T. de Chan, Wing-tsit and Watson, B. (eds.), *Sources of Chinese Tradition*, Columbia University Press, New York, 1961.

Bary, W. T. de, Hay, S. N., Weiler, R. and Yarrow, A., *Sources of Indian Tradition*, Columbia University Press, New York, 1964.

Bary, W. T. de and Embree, A. T. (eds.), *Approaches to Asian Civilization*, Columbia University Press, New York, 1964.

Blanchard, W., *Thailand*, Human Relations Area Files Press, Yale, New Haven, 1958.

Blau, P. M., *The Dynamics of Bureaucracy*, University of Chicago Press, Chicago, 1966.

BMF Committee of Enquiry Final Report, Bank Bumiputra Malaysia Berhad, Kuala Lumpur, 1986, vol. 2.

Braibanti, Ralph, 'Reflections on Bureaucratic Corruption', *Public Administration*, Royal Institute of Public Administration, London, 1962 vol. 40, no. 4.

Braibanti, R., *Research on the Bureaucracy of Pakistan*, Duke University Press, Durham, North Carolina, 1966.

Brasz, H. A., 'Some Notes on the Sociology of Corruption', *Sociologia Neerlandica*, Netherlands Sociological Society, Assen, 1963, vol. 1, no. 2.

Bronowski, J., *Science and Human Values*, Julian Messner, New York, 1956.

Carino, Ledevina V., 'The Definition of Graft and Corruption and the Conflict of Ethics and Law', *Philippine Journal of Public Administration*, July–October 1979, vol. XXIII, nos. 3 and 4.

Cerf, Christopher and Albee, Marina, *Small Fires*, Summit Books, New York, 1990.

Cicero, *The Verrine Orations*, tr. L. H. G. Greenwood, Heinemann, London, 1935, vol. 1, 44, no. 116.

Corpuz, O. D., *The Bureaucracy in the Philippines*, Institute of Public Administration, University of the Philippines, 1957.

Djamester A. Simarmata, *Reformasi Ekonomi Menurut Undang-Undang Dasar 1945*, Centre for Policy and Implementation Studies, Jakarta, 1998.

Douglass, P. H., *Ethics in Government*, Harvard University Press, Cambridge, Mass., 1952.

Dwivedi, O. P. 'Bureaucratic Corruption in Developing Countries', *Asian Survey*, Institute of International Studies, University of California, Berkeley, April 1967, vol. VII, no. 4.

Fakir Jany Muhammad Asaad, *Akhlak-I-Falaly*, tr. W. F. Thompson, Mustafai Press, Lahore, 1895.

Feuer, Lewis E. (ed.), *Marx and Engels*, Doubleday, New York, 1959.

Furnivall, J. S., *Colonial Policy and Practice*, New York University Press, New York, 1956.

Goodwin, Michael, *Nineteenth Century Opinion*, Penguin Books, London, 1951.

Gorbachov, Mikhail, 'On Organization and the Party's Personnel Policy', Report of the General Secretary of the CPSU Central Committee, 27 January 1987.

Greenstone, J. D., 'Corruption and Self Interest in Kampala and Nairobi: A Comment on Local Politics in Africa', *Comparative Studies in Society and History*, Mouton, The Hague, 1965–6, vol. VIII.

Gupta, B. B., 'Santhanam Committee Report: An Appraisal', *The Modern Review*, Prabasi Press, Calcutta, 6 December 1964, vol. CXVI, no. 6.

Gwyn, W. B., *Democracy and the Cost of Politics in Britain*, Athlone Press, London, 1962.

Haggard, Howard W., *Devils, Drugs and Doctors*, Pocket Books, New York, 1959.

Halayya, M., *Emergency: A War on Corruption*, S. Chand, New Delhi, 1978.

Heidenheimer, Arnold J. (ed.), *Political Corruption*, Holt, Rheinbart and Winston, New York, 1970.

Hiskett, M., 'Kitab al-Farq: A Work on the Habe Kingdoms Attributed to Uthman and Fodio', *Bulletin of the School of Oriental and African Studies*, University of London, London, 1960, vol. 23.

Huizinga, J., *Men and Ideas*, tr. J. S. Holmes and H. van Marle, Meridian Books, New York, 1959.

Ibn Khaldun, *The Muqaddimah*, tr. F. Rosenthal, Routledge and Kegan Paul, London, 1958 (3 vols.).

Kai Kans ibn Iskandar, *A Mirror for Princes*, tr. R. Levy, Crescent Press, London, 1951.

Kaplan, Justin, *Lincoln Steffens*, Jonathan Cape, London, 1975.

Katib Chelebi, *The Balance of Truth*, tr. Lewis, Allen and Unwin, London, 1957.

Khan, E., *Anecdotes from Islam*, Ashraf Publications, Lahore, 1947.

Kompas, Jakarta, 28 September 1983, 29 September 1983.

Kulwant Singh, 'The Working of Jammu and Kashmir Prevention of Corruption Acts: An Empirical Study', *Journal of the Indian Law Institute*, 1987, vol. 29:3.

LaPalambara, J. (ed.), *Bureaucracy and Political Development*, Princeton University Press, New Jersey, 1963.

Lasswell, H. D., 'Bribery', *Encyclopedia of the Social Sciences*, Macmillan, New York, 1960, vols. I–II.

Lavince, E. H., *Stand and Deliver*, I Routledge, London, 1931.

Lee Kuan Yew, *The Singapore Story*, Times Editions, Singapore, 1998.

Lee, Rance P. L. (ed.), *Corruption and Its Control in Hong Kong*, The Chinese University Press, Hong Kong, 1981.

Leff, N. H., 'Economic Development through Bureaucratic Corruption', *The American Behavioral Scientist*, Metron, New York, November 1964, vol. VIII, no. 3.

Leys, Colin, 'What is the Problem about Corruption?', *The Journal of Modern African Studies*, Cambridge University Press, London, August 1965, vol. 3 no. 2.

Lim Chong Yah, 'The Malayan Rubber Replanting Taxes', *The Malayan Economic Review*, Malayan Economic Society, Singapore, October 1961, vol. VI, no. 2.

Lim Kit Siang, 'The BMF Scandal, Kuala Lumpur, 1983', Speech in Parliament, 24 October 1983.

McMullan, A., 'A Theory of Corruption', *The Sociological Review*, University of Keele, Staffordshire, July 1961, vol. IX, no. 2.

Malaysia Official Yearbook, 1964, Government Printing Press, Kuala Lumpur, 1966.

Malaysian Digest, Kuala Lumpur, 15 January 1984, vol. 15, no. 1.

Marx, Karl and Engels, Frederick, *Collected Works*, Progress Publishers, Moscow, 1979. *On Religion*, Progress Publishers, Moscow, 1966.

Mauss, Marcel, *The Gift*, tr. I. Cunnison, Cohen and West, London, 1954.

Mez, A., *The Renaissance of Islam*, tr. S. K. Baksh and D. S. Margoliouth, Jubilee Publishing House, Patna, 1937.

Mitures, Primitivo, *The Conjugal Dictatorship of Ferdinand and Imelda Marcos I*, Union Square Publications, San Francisco, 1986.

Mkandawire, Thandika and Olukoshi, Adebayo (eds.), *Between Liberalisation and Oppression*, Codesria, Dakar, Senegal, 1995.

Mohammad Hatta, *The Co-operative Movement in Indonesia*, Cornell University Press, Ithaca, 1957.

Montgomery, J. D. and Siffin, W. J. (eds.), *Approaches to Development*, McGraw-Hill, New York, 1966.

Murtada Mutahhari, *Attitude and Conduct of Prophet Muhammad*, tr. H.V. Dastjerdi, Islamic Propagation Organization, Tehran, 1968.

——, *Polarization around the Character of Ali Ibn Abi Talib*, tr. from Persian, World Organization for Islamic Services, 1981.

Narendra K. Singhi, *Bureaucracy: Positions and Persons*, Abhinav Publications, New Delhi, 1974.

Neely, Richard, 'The Politics of Crime', *The Atlantic Monthly*, USA, August 1982.

The New Straits Times, Kuala Lumpur, 12 September 1983, 8 January 1985, 12 March 1986, 28 June 1986.

Nghiem Dang, *Vietnam, Politics and Public Administration*, East–West Center Press, Honolulu, 1966.

Nizam al-Mulk, *The Book of Government or Rules for Kings*, tr. H. Drake, Routledge and Kegan Paul, London, 1960.

Noggle, B., *The Teapot Dome*, Louisiana State University Press, Baton Rouge, 1962.

Nye, J. S., 'Corruption and Political Development: A Cost Benefit Analaysis', *The American Political Science Review*, American Political Science Association, Washington, June 1967, vol. LXI, no. 2.

O'Leary, C., *The Elimination of Corrupt Practices in British Elections 1868–1911*, Oxford University Press, London, 1962.

The Pakistan Times Overseas Weekly, Lahore, 10 June 1984, 17 June 1984, 24 June 1984, 7 April 1985, 29 September 1985, 22 December 1985, 12 January 1986, 2 March 1986, 3 August 1986, 10 August 1986, 17 August 1986, 31 August 1986.

Patton, H. J., *Ahmad ibn Hanbal and the Mihna*, Brill, Leiden, 1897.

Payne, Robert, *The Corrupt Society*, Praeger Publishers, New York, 1975.

Rashid, A., *Corruption in Pakistan*, 1965.

Reiger, C. C., *The Era of the Muckrakers*, Peter Smith, Gloucester, Mass., 1957.

Report of the Auditor-Geneal, Federal Government, Malaysia, 1977, Kuala Lumpur, 1980.

Report of the Commission of Inquiry into Corrupt, Illegal or Undersirable Practices at Elections, Singapore Legislative Assembly, Sessional papers, no. cmd, 7 of 1958, Government Printing Office, Singapore, 1958.

Report of the Commission of Inquiry into the $500,000 Bank Account of Mr Chew Swee Kee and the Income Tax Department Leakage in connection therewith, Singapore Government, Government Printing Office, Singapore, 1959.

Report of a Commission to enquire into Matters affecting the Integrity of the Public Services, 1955, Federation of Malaya, Government Printing Press, Kuala Lumpur, 1955.

Report of the Committee on the Prevention of Corruption, Ministry of Home Affairs, Government of India, New Delhi, n.d.

Riggs, F. W., *Administration in Developing Countries*, Houghton Miflin, Boston, 1964.

———, *Thailand*, East–West Center Press, Honolulu, 1966.

Ritter, G., *The Corrupting Influence of Power*, tr. F. W. Pick, Tower Bridge Publications, Essex, 1952.

Rogow, A. A. and Lasswell, H. D., *Power, Corruption and Rectitude*, Prentice Hall, New Jersey, 1963.

SADACHAR — *Movement for Purity in National Life*, Ministry of Information and Broadcasting, Government of India, New Delhi, 1964.

Salter, J. T., *Boss Rule*, Whittlesey House, New York, 1935.

Sari Mehmed Pasha, *Ottoman Statecraft*, tr. W .L. Wright, Princeton University Press, Princeton, 1936.

Senturia, J. J., 'Political Corruption', *Encyclopedia of the Social Sciences*, Macmillan, New York, 1960, vols. 3–4.

Shakib Arsalan, *Our Decline and Its Causes*, tr. M. A. Shakoor, Ashraf, Lahore, 1952.

Shaykh Muhammad Jawad Mughniyyah, *The Despotic Rulers*, tr. M. Fazal Haq, Islamic Seminary Publications, Karachi, 1985.

Sinar Harapan, Djakarta, 11 August 1967, 28 August 1967, 3 September 1967, 6 September 1967, 7 September 1967, 16 September 1967.

Smith, M. G., 'Historical and Cultural Conditions of Political Corruption among the Hausa', *Comparative Studies in Society and History*, Mouton, The Hague, 1963–4, vol. 6.

Sorokin, P. A. and Lunden, W. A., *Power and Morality*, Porter Sargent, Boston, 1959.

Spiro, H. J., *Politics in Africa*, Prentice Hall, New Jersey, 1962.

The Star, Kuala Lumpur, 12 September 1983, 17 October 1983, 17 June 1986, 27 June 1986.

The Straits Times, Kuala Lumpur and Singapore, 20 May 1967, 1 June 1967, 5 June 1967, 14 June 1967, 16 June 1967, 17 June 1967, 22 June 1967, 13 March 1986, 22 April 1986, 17 May 1986.

The Sunday Mail, Kuala Lumpur and Singapore, 28 May 1967.

Suresh Kohli (ed.), *Corruption in India*, Chetana Publications, New Delhi, 1978.

Syed Hussein Alatas, 'Asia Needs a Strong Sense of Shame', *The Asian Wall Street Journal*, Hong Kong, 8 December 1980.

——, *Corruption: Its Nature, Causes and Functions*, Gower Publishing Company, Aldershot, England, Brookfield, USA, 1990.

——, 'Effects of Corruption', *Singapore Tiger Standard*, Singapore, 28 February 1957.

——, 'Feudalism in Malaysian Society: A Study in Historical Continuity', International Conference on Asian History, Kuala Lumpur, Paper, August 1960, no. 110.

——, *Intellectuals in Developing Societies*, Frank Cass, London, 1977.

——, 'Ke arah Integrasi Nasional', *Kertas Kerja* (Working Paper), Khemah Kerja Politik Barisan Nasional, Morib, Selangor, 1–3 February 1986.

——, 'Korupsi Apa Yang Bisa Diperbuat' (Report of interview), *Tempo*, 30 July 1983.

——, 'Moral Awakening Needed to End Corruption in Asia', *The Asian Wall Street Journal*, Hong Kong, 25 February 1981.

——, 'Sense of Pride and Shame', *Saudi Gazette*, Jeddah, 21–22 May 1981.

——, 'Some Fundamental Problems of Colonialism', *Eastern World*, London, November 1956.

——, *Sosiologi Korupsi*, LP3S, Jakarta, 1981.

——, 'The Grading of Occupational Prestige Amongst the Malays in Malaysia', paper delivered at the International Conference on Comparative Social Research, New Delhi, 27 March–1 April 1967.

——, *The Myth of the Lazy Native*, Frank Cass, London, 1977.

——, *The Problem of Corruption*, Times Books International, Singapore, 1986.

——, 'The Sociology of Graft', *Asia Magazine*, Tokyo, 9 February 1969.

——, *Thomas Stamford Raffles: Schemer or Reformer?*, Angus and Robertson, Sydney, 1971.

Syed Moinul Haq, *Hadrat Abu Bakar*, Ashraf Publications, Lahore, 1947.

Tan Teow Yeow, 'Checks against Maladministration within the Administration Itself', paper delivered at the Southeast Asian and Australasian Law Students Seminar on the Rule of Law in a Developing Nation, Singapore, 9–12 May 1967.

Tranperency International News Letter, Berlin, March 1997.

Tsunoda R., Bary, W. T. de, and Keene, D., *Sources of Japanese Tradition*, Columbia University Press, New York, 1961.

Utusan Malaysia, Kuala Lumpur, 12 September 1983.

Wafaqi Mohtasib (Ombudsman)'s Annual Report for 1983, Islamabad, 1984.

Wafaqi Mohtasib (Ombudsman)'s Annual Report for 1984, Islamabad, 1985.

Wang An Shih, 'Memorial of a Myriad Words' (Wan Yen Shu), in H. R. Williamson, *Wang An Shih*, A. Probsthain, London, 1935, vol. 2.

Weiner, Myron, *The Politics of Scarcity*, University of Chicago Press, Chicago, 1962.

Wertheim, W. F., *East–West Parallels*, Quadrangle Books, Chicago, 1965.

Wiese, L. von and Becker, H., *Systematic Sociology*, John Wiley, New York, 1932.

Wraith, R. and Simpkins, E., *Corruption in Developing Countries*, Allen and Unwin, London, 1963.

Yanaga, C., *Japanese People and Politics*, John Wiley, New York, 1956.

INDEX